SOFT
IS THE
NEW
HARD

How to Communicate Effectively
Under Pressure

LEAH METHER

© Leah Mether 2019

First published in 2019 by Methmac Communications Pty Ltd.
All rights reserved.

No part of this publication may be reproduced by any means
without written prior consent of the publisher.

This book uses personal stories and examples from clients to highlight
key points. Names have been changed to protect individual privacy.

Every effort has been made to trace and acknowledge the original
source of material used within this book. Where the attempt has
been unsuccessful, the publisher would be pleased to hear from the
author/publisher to rectify any omission.

Edited by Kath Walters.

Typset by Liz Seymour, Seymour Designs.

Printed and bound by Ingram Sparks.

National Library of Australia Cataloguing-in-Publication entry

Title: Soft is the New Hard

Subtitle: How to Communicate Effectively Under Pressure

ISBN: -13: 978-0-6484845-0-9 (paperback)

Subjects: Business, communication, soft skills, leadership.

PRAISE FOR SOFT IS THE NEW HARD

"This book is a masterclass in communication. Packed with case studies, stories and research it has a perfect blend of anecdote and data. Soft is indeed the new hard, and sometimes it's real hard. But as Leah has shown with succinct and elegantly simple concepts, it's a skill that can be learned. Full of many eye-opening, "wow!", moments and many, more reassuring "phew, it's not just me" moments, this isn't just a book for leaders, it's a book for life.

Rachael Robertson, Antarctic Expedition Leader, Leadership Expert and Author of *Leading on the Edge: Extraordinary Stories and Leadership Insights from the World's Most Extreme Workplace*

"If you are a leader who wants to be heard in the 21st century, this book decodes the future of communications."

Oscar Trimboli - Author & Award Winning Podcaster of Deep Listening

"I wish I'd had this book as a reference when I started my leadership career. I'm glad it's been written now. This will be a go-to book in my organisational leadership and coaching practice. I'll be buying it for many of my clients. There are so many concepts in here that I value, it's hard to choose one. Yet this, for me, sums up the book **"Respect is everything as a leader. And to get it, you need to communicate in a way that connects."** If you want to ensure you're on top of your communication game, you simply must read this book.

Maree McPherson, Leadership and Executive Coach, Professional Mentor, and Author of *Cutting Through the Grass Ceiling: Women Creating Possibility in Regional Australia*

"In 'Soft is the New Hard', Leah has created a very practical guide that gives all of us the opportunity to become more effective communicators under pressure. Being aware of what drives and motivates us and influences our choices in communication, enables all of us to step into a conversation in a very different way. Understanding our own impact and taking 'control' of the choices we make and the way in which we engage others, creates very different outcomes – ones that enable us to move forward and remain 'above the line'. The compelling stories that she shares throughout the book and the practical examples offered for us to test and explore also make this content very real and current. We are looking forward to continuing to use it ourselves and recommending it to others."

Gayle Hardie and Malcolm Lazenby, Co-Founders,
Global Leadership Foundation.

"'Soft is the New Hard' is a personal coaching session on how to improve your own communication in order to improve your success and satisfaction in your workplace. A must read for all leaders and aspiring leaders."

Sally Neenan, team leader

I sincerely love this book. I feel like I knew soft skills were important but now I really understand the impact they have in so many different environments. I am confidently walking away with an action plan (the five C's) that I can easily reference as needed. I will happily read this multiple times."

Robyn Wildblood, program support manager

ABOUT THE AUTHOR

Leah Mether helps people get out of their own way with the development of soft skills.

She is a speaker, trainer, coach, facilitator and author known for her direct, enthusiastic and relatable style.

With a background in leadership, corporate communications and journalism, Leah works with executives, leaders and employees across Australia to help them improve their communication and self-management.

Her work is based on the belief that soft skills are the new hard; we are our own biggest roadblock to success; and no-one is a perfect communicator, everyone can improve.

Leah lives in the small town of Willow Grove in Gippsland, Victoria; overlooking Blue Rock Lake and the Baw Baw ranges.

She is the mother of three energetic sons and a dedicated community volunteer.

DEDICATION

To Mum and Dad, for giving me such strong foundations.
And to my boys. I hope I'm laying solid foundations for you.

CONTENTS

Chapter 8 **COURAGE**   **132**

INTRODUCTION

Don't let the name 'soft skills' fool you; soft skills are not easy. Skills like communication, emotional intelligence, resilience, leadership, teamwork, empathy, mindset, problem solving and adaptability. They're what make someone good to work with, not simply good at what they do. Soft skills are often more difficult to master than 'hard' job-specific technical skills that require years of formal study or work experience. Yet they are essential to personal and career success.

Of all the soft skills, communication tops the food chain. Look at any job advertisement or position description and you will likely find communication listed as an 'essential skill' in the selection criteria. It's paramount in any role that involves working with other people – in short, every leadership role.

Communication is especially important when you're in high pressure situations, such as:

► leading a team through a restructure or transition

► labouring under a heavy workload

► dealing with technology, regulatory or procedural changes within an organisation

► facing tight deadlines, an emergency or crisis

► delivering a difficult message

► experiencing conflict with colleagues or bosses.

Yet it's a skill many people lack.

So why does no one prepare you for how hard the 'soft' part of leadership and interpersonal relationships are? Why does no one tell you the hardest part of working in a team is the people bit, particularly at times of high pressure, stress or conflict?

This is the question I'm often asked by frustrated clients after failed communication with a team member or colleague. This is the question I asked myself too, until I decided to do something about it by learning more about how to improve my soft skills and step up for success. Then I began teaching people the very same techniques that worked for me.

The problem is, most people believe you're either born a good communicator or you're not, and that if you can speak and listen, you can communicate. This misguided belief – that communication skills are inherent and not dependent on acquired knowledge – means communications training is lacking from mainstream education. It's not part of school curriculums and it's not standard in most workplaces.

In fact, active development of communication skills is often neglected entirely, leaving people to muddle through on their own in a sink-or-swim approach.

This disregard for what is an essential career (and life) skill leaves many people too embarrassed to admit they're struggling. They worry their challenges show they have an inherent incapacity to communicate. They do not.

The good news is, like all skills, communication can be developed and you have to start with the foundations first.

That's why I've written this book – to teach you the foundations that underpin effective communication. Foundations that, if I had my way, would be taught in every school and reinforced in every workplace throughout the world. That's how important this is.

Over the last decade, I've worked with thousands of people – leaders, managers, executives and employees – struggling to communicate effectively under pressure and unsure about what to do about it.

People like you.

People who may be successful, competent and confident but know their communication skills could be improved.

People who are frustrated they can't motivate, influence and persuade people the way they'd like.

People under intense pressure trying hard to stay calm but finding their emotional responses get in the way.

People who struggle to get their point across in a way that connects, or flounder when put on the spot.

People who want to improve the way they communicate but are not sure how to make it happen or where to start.

Some of you may have attended communications training before or read a book on the topic, but it hasn't hit the mark. While you may have made changes in the immediate aftermath, you quickly fell back into old habits. You know what you need to do, but you don't seem to be able to do it.

And now you've ended up here, with this book. You're probably wondering if it's going to be like all the others. I can tell you, it's not.

This book does more than teach you flash-in-the-pan communication skills. It will teach you a way of looking at communication and managing yourself that has the power to change your life. That's not overstating it. How do I know? Because the steps outlined in this book changed my life and have changed the lives of many of my clients. Now, I hope they'll change yours too.

But who am I to give you advice on communication?

Well, let me first tell you who I'm not.

I'm not here to impress you. I won't bore you with big words, complex theories, dry facts, figures and studies. I'm here to help you get results. I want nothing more than for you to succeed and I know from experience that compassionate honesty is the best way to help you get there. So I'm not going to fluff around; I'll be direct, real and use plain speak.

Nor am I a psychologist. I'm not going to lecture you on the intricacies of how the human brain works. That's not my expertise either.

What I am is a communications specialist with 15 years' practical experience working with people from a broad range of backgrounds, industries, professions and positions. I have worked with executives in government agencies, leaders and employees in large corporate and industrial settings, trades supervisors, professionals, school teachers, students, small business owners, staff and more.

I've coached and trained thousands of people under intense personal and professional stress. These are people leading business transition and significant industrial change; leaders delivering difficult messages in a time of crisis; employees struggling with aggressive managers; and those starting out on their career paths, who find themselves in toxic work environments.

One message has come through loud and clear from my work with clients. It is this: regardless of your position, success, confidence or competence, soft skills are hard and people are desperate to know how to make them easier.

That's where this book comes in. In these pages, I share my knowledge and proven strategies that will help you develop your communication capability in a new and different way.

This book offers you a complete solution; a step-by-step process that underpins communication. It's about laying the foundations to ensure that when you do communicate, you do it effectively. It's about managing yourself first in order to manage your communication with others.

Like most things in life, the pay-off is the greatest if you're prepared to play a long game, get uncomfortable and do the work. The steps laid out in this book are simple but not easy, and they require a commitment to being and doing better. Developing your communication skills is a continual process of self-improvement, not an end game.

But I guarantee you the steps outlined in these pages work. If you're prepared to put them into practice, your communication will improve dramatically and transform your effectiveness as a leader – and not only when the going's easy. These steps will help you sail through the storm of interpersonal relationships steady and true.

Leah

Chapter 1

DO YOU HAVE A PEOPLE PROBLEM?

Sarah was smart, driven and confident. A high achiever promoted into her first leadership role in a male-dominated industry. She was ready. She was enthusiastic. She had great ideas and aspirations to lift her team from one that merely met baseline expectations to one that excelled. Yet, here she was, sitting in front of me, completely deflated.

"Why does no one prepare you for how hard the people part of leadership is?" she asked. "All I want is for the people in my team to be the best they can be. I want to inspire them to strive for success and improvement like I do. But it's not working. They're not engaged at all and don't seem interested in what I have to say. I really don't know what to do."

Sarah is typical of the many new leaders who come to me for help. Promoted for her excellent technical skills and experience, she quickly felt out of her depth when trying to manage her team, which was made up of people with very different personalities to hers. She struggled to relate to them and couldn't understand their lack of personal drive.

Until she became a leader, the people side of her work had come easily to her. In previous roles, she had worked with people of a similar age, with similar goals. In this new position with a new company, her circumstances were quite different. Her staff were older than her and had many more years' experience. They were happy coasting through their work days and didn't like being told what to do. Their motivations were very different to hers.

Many leaders face a similar situation to the one Sarah confronted. No matter how strong your interpersonal skills are, at some point in your life, you will find someone you struggle to get along with. Personalities clash, difficult decisions are made, and circumstances outside your control lead to stress, heightened emotions, conflict and confusion.

It's happened to me. It's almost certainly happened to you. And it's also happened to many of my clients. Clients like Sarah.

Sarah's experience brought back memories of my first professional leadership role. I was communications manager of a government organisation, yet I struggled to communicate with a member of my team. What I said just didn't connect with this person. When I tried to motivate and encourage her, she disengaged. When I provided constructive feedback, she became defensive. She let her day-to-day emotions dictate how she treated colleagues and affect her performance. While she was good at the technical side of her role, she struggled to build relationships.

Here I was – managing communications for a 200-person organisation, developing key messages for a $230 million project, engaging with a customer base of 55,000 people, liaising with government and relating well with all other staff – and my most difficult challenge was within my own team, from someone who was meant to help make my job easier. It was embarrassing and infuriating. Her performance felt like a reflection on my leadership. And I had no idea how to solve it.

HOW DID IT COME TO THIS?

Does this sound familiar? You're smart. Competent. Capable. You've got the experience and technical skills to do your job. You know your stuff. But when it comes to some people on your team, you feel out of your depth. You struggle to connect, and nothing you try seems to be working. You feel like you're spinning out of control.

You might be holding it together on the surface but underneath you're paddling madly to stay afloat. It's only a matter of time before you lose your temper. Your emotions are all over the place and you feel like you're failing.

The communication problems you're having with your colleagues, boss or team are not only affecting your performance, they're affecting you personally. You're fighting to stay positive and upbeat, but your frustration and anger are breaking through. Your performance, effectiveness and efficiency may be suffering.

If it goes on like this, your position could well be in trouble. You're doing your best but you're barely hanging on and it takes all your energy to pull yourself together to get through the day. You're sinking, not swimming. Floundering, not flourishing.

You may feel angry with yourself. You go into conversations intending to stay calm but your emotions and those of other people derail your intentions. You know what you want to say but can't get it out – or if you do, it's not connecting. You know the result you want, but you're not getting it. You know you need help, you know something has to change. But what and how?

You go home exhausted, emotionally and mentally drained. You've got nothing left for your partner, family or friends. The communication problems you're experiencing at work are now starting to flow through into your personal life as well. You're snappy, brooding, short-tempered and highly stressed. You know you're not always nice to be around. In fact, you're falling into those very same behaviours you're trying to stop in your team.

Something's got to give.

Imposter syndrome is creeping into your subconsciousness. 'Maybe I'm not cut out for this,' the little voice of self-doubt whispers. 'Perhaps I should look for another job?' Perhaps, but probably not. See, if you don't address this, if you don't develop strategies to help improve your communication, this same situation – or one just like it – will probably emerge in your next role. If not immediately, then eventually.

So how the hell did it come to this? Why do you have a 'people problem'?

For most leaders, people problems come as a shock. It's not like you can't communicate. You know how to hold a conversation. You wouldn't be in the job if you didn't have decent communication skills. You're approachable. You're passionate. But you've tried the tools from your usual bag of tricks and they're not cutting it this time.

The more you try to engage with people, the more they seem to disengage from you. Why isn't your message getting through? Why is there resistance? Why are people still not getting it? You feel misunderstood, and everything you say seems to be taken the wrong way.

It shouldn't be this hard. Surely communication and managing relationships shouldn't be the most difficult part of your job? Yet here you are. And you're not alone.

HOW PEOPLE PROBLEMS DEVELOP

Lucas was an experienced leader with a long history in the power industry when he received a promotion. Lucas considered his people skills a strength. He had led many teams to success in the past and was confident he'd be able to handle a new position with a new team. It was a big surprise to him when he found he couldn't.

Within weeks of taking up his new role, he felt like he was leading kindergarten kids rather than qualified adults. They openly challenged him in morning pre-start briefings by questioning his instructions. They talked back and complained whenever they were asked to do something they didn't want to do. They were defiant and aggressive. Some threw tantrums like toddlers when he approached them on the job to deliver basic feedback, exploding with anger, yelling, abusing and swearing. Others were more manipulative and tried to undermine him by talking behind his back and spreading rumours.

It was a disaster. Lucas had a people problem and while his case might be one of the more extreme I've come across, it's certainly not isolated.

So why does it happen? Why can't we all just get along? The answer is humans are driven by complex motivations and respond to pressure in different ways. While our intention is rarely to be a difficult person, our fears can make us selfish, defensive and emotionally reactive. To some extent, we're all driven by our own personal agendas, beliefs and truths, often without realising it. Even those of us who are kind and considerate of other people's needs and viewpoints are the centre of our own universe, the hero in our own story, and look at the world through our own lens.

The problem is, we forget other people have a different lens to us. We forget that personality, upbringing, and experience make us unique and that no-one else thinks exactly like us. No-one. Even people with similar values and backgrounds will not share our way of thinking completely. That means relating to other people – even those we get along with – can be more difficult than we expect.

On top of this, we live in an age of technical disruption where pressure at work to adapt and adjust is increasing and, alongside it, pressure to be able to communicate well with others, particularly in challenging and changing environments. In my experience, most leaders can communicate well enough when there is plenty of time, minimal conflict, and low pressure, but when the going gets tough – like it did for Lucas – we need to find new ways to connect and get our message across.

Too often, pressure sees us resort to four common automatic and emotional responses: deny, blame, justify and defend.

We say things like:

"No, I don't do that." (Deny)

"Well, I do communicate like that but it's their fault." (Blame)

"I do communicate aggressively but that's the culture of my workplace, so it's ok." (Justify)

"No, there's no problem. Everything's fine. You're the one with the problem, not me." (Defend)

When we or others fall into these automatic responses, people problems form.

And while we often see other people as the problem, it's important to remember that we are part of the problem too. People problems don't exist separately to us. In later chapters I'll explore this idea in detail, but for now I want you to think about when you're stuck in traffic. Do you get frustrated and complain about all the cars around you, hitting the steering wheel and swearing at 'the damn traffic', or do you remember that you are part of the traffic too and someone in another car is probably saying the same thing about you? Never forget – the traffic is not separate to you; you are the traffic.

PORTRAIT OF A PEOPLE PROBLEM

Here are some of the most common problems that leaders report when they come to me for help. Often these problems are with their staff, although sometimes they're with their own leader or with their peers and management colleagues.

People problems:

1. Passive resistance

Saying yes to something, but not doing it. Missing deadlines and meetings. Letting you as leader make mistakes that could have been prevented. Lacking engagement and contribution. Not letting you know about problems until they are out of control, such as not warning you about project overruns.

Communication styles: Passive, passive-aggressive

2. Insubordination and undermining

Talking back, talking when you are speaking, interrupting and constantly raising objections. Predicting failure without evidence and presenting problems without solutions. Talking behind your back and undermining your decision or character. Spreading rumours or falsehoods. Turning up late to meetings without explanation. Muttering in meetings but not actually speaking up. Leaving meetings and raising objections with peers who do not have decision-making responsibility.

Communication styles: Aggressive, passive-aggressive

3. Lack of productivity and laziness

Not working as expected. Blaming others when mistakes are made and justifying poor performance. Arriving late to work, taking long lunch breaks and taking advantage of flexible working arrangements. Avoiding tasks that are not strictly within their role. Leaving tasks to others in the team. Taking days off. Lack of decision making. Endless meetings without resolution.

Communication styles: This behaviour is not directly related to a communication style, although it's likely the offender will be passive, passive-aggressive or aggressive

4. Avoidance

Avoiding challenges, feedback, difficult conversations, problems and conflict. Staying silent on important issues and letting them escalate or continue unchecked.

Communication styles: Passive

5. Incompetence

Making mistakes repeatedly. Not learning from mistakes. Not taking any initiative. Getting simple tasks wrong. Blaming others. Refusing to resolve problems with colleagues. Refusing to attend meetings. Not doing, or being unable to complete, the basics of a role.

Communication styles: Can be passive, passive-aggressive or aggressive

6. Conflict

Picking fights and escalating disagreements to arguments. Rudeness. Swearing. Shouting. Taking industrial action without first seeking resolution. Getting involved in other people's conflicts. Stirring up feelings of concern or anger.

Communication styles: Aggressive

If you've experienced one or more of these problems, you've probably already tried to solve it. You may have even had success in raising the issue, or having a conversation to address it. But for some reason your approach didn't resolve the issue and your people problem grew. Now you're frustrated and not sure of your next step. The reality is, being able to communicate under the pressure of a people problem requires a whole new skill set and my aim is to teach it to you, while also explaining why your existing knowledge and training may have been failing you just when you need it most.

THE SINKING SHIP

"If you want to know why so many organisations sink into chaos, look no further than their leaders' mouths," John Hamm wrote in his article 'The Five Messages Leaders Must Manage', published in the May 2006 issue of *Harvard Business Review*.

The impact of poor communication can be that severe.

I've seen the CEO of a large organisation lose the respect of an entire workforce based on his poor communication skills. This man was incredibly intelligent but socially awkward – and this was his undoing. His lack of basic interpersonal skills had a significant impact on his success.

Even the way he walked through the corridors of the building got people off-side. How? Because he walked with his head bent down, eyes fixed firmly on the floor in front of him, giving those he walked past no acknowledgment. No smile. No hello. No greeting at all. And the workforce hated it. 'Rude' they called him. 'Arrogant.' 'Too up himself to even say good morning.' This perception of staff wasn't the intention of the leader, but it was the result of his behaviour.

Poor communication – whether you're on the giving or receiving end – can also have serious impacts on your health. In extreme cases, it can be the catalyst for emotional breakdowns.

That's what happened to Kate, who phoned me in tears after walking out of a management meeting two months into her new job. She was at breaking point already, pushed to the edge by an aggressive boss whose unrealistic demands and micromanaging nature wore her down from a highly competent manager to a shell of the person she'd been when she started.

Kate was good at her job. She knew her stuff. But under the charge of a bullying boss who attacked whenever challenged, Kate was crumbling. It wasn't just Kate's performance that was suffering but her health too. The worst part was, Kate could feel herself starting to 'live down' to her boss's poor expectations of her, rather than up to the standard she knew she was really at herself.

"I don't know what to do," Kate said. "She doesn't value anything I say."

Kate needed a strategy to deal with the situation. Her boss wasn't going to change, so she was left with two choices – change her response to her boss or leave.

Lucas was at a similar breaking point but from another perspective – it was he who had turned into the aggressive and explosive manager. His team was out of control and he used this to justify the wild swings of his emotional responses. His staff were aggressive, rude, manipulative and showed a total disregard for his leadership. So Lucas retaliated by fighting fire with fire.

The stress was evident on his face and in his body language when he sat across from me in a coaching session. His movements were jerky, the bags under his eyes dark purple, and the skin around it blotchy. His hands almost shook as he rubbed them up and down his face. This was a man at the point of emotional collapse. When I looked at him, my first thought was: no one can ever tell me soft skills aren't hard.

Lucas needed to take action. He needed strategies to implement and he needed them now. Lucas wanted a quick fix and I didn't blame him. He wanted things to get better – fast, before something really bad happened. He knew carrying on like this wasn't sustainable. He also knew that his bosses were watching closely, and he knew his career was well and truly under threat.

But while Lucas thought he needed a quick coaching session to help him have difficult conversations and then all would be fixed, my message to him was clear: this wasn't about other people, it was about him, and in order to manage his people, he first needed to manage himself. He had to get the foundations right to be able to communicate effectively under pressure.

The personal and professional toll that Lucas and Kate both faced highlights the repercussions of not laying those foundations first. Struggling to communicate under pressure can lead to a terrible waste of talent and have a tremendous impact on your mental and physical health, as well as your job performance. But the good news is, it doesn't have to be that way.

My research, personal experimentation, and the practical experience of my clients is clear. If you take the steps outlined in this book and lay the foundations of communication before you open your mouth, you will take your leadership and your career to the next level. You will reduce the pressure you face, improve your performance when the going gets tough, and foster a healthier more productive workforce as a result. My aim is to change the way you think about communication forever.

Chapter 2

COMMUNICATING UNDER PRESSURE

When you have a people problem, your communication is automatically under pressure. It's the reason why you can suddenly hit a communications wall after years of thinking you had excellent people skills. The higher up the ladder you go, the more pressure you face. You make critical decisions, you delegate more, and your remuneration is tied to the results you deliver. At the same time, fewer people give you honest feedback when you get it wrong.

Many leaders also fall into the trap of thinking they 'know' how to communicate and forget that it's something we all have to constantly work on improving.

A person's ability to communicate well doesn't necessarily correlate with how smart, educated or experienced they are. We all know people who are highly intelligent and technically brilliant but struggle with interpersonal skills. While they might reach a high level in their career or be promoted on the back of their 'hard' technical skills, eventually the lack of soft skills is their undoing.

I've seen it many times: Senior executives and leaders who stumble and sometimes crumble, not because they're not smart enough, but because they don't understand how to communicate effectively. In the end, it's those pesky 'soft' skills – the capabilities they may have dismissed as frivolous and unimportant – that hinder their success.

Here's the thing: No-one is a perfect communicator, everyone can improve. Whether you're a CEO or new starter, an executive or first-time leader, everyone can do better and no-one gets it right all the time. Improving your communication is a process, not an end result. While your instincts might carry you through in low pressure situations, when the pressure is on, the cracks or deficiencies in your communication are highlighted. Even those who have a natural ability to communicate well need to up their game from time to time.

The good news is that communication is a skill. And, like all skills, you can improve it if you learn and practice. Regardless of your position or skill level, if you want to step up, go further, future-proof your employability, and have more success in your career and relationships, developing your communication skills is something you must invest your time in. And take it from me, that investment is worthwhile.

MY STORY

It was 2014 and I was mother to a three-month-old baby and two toddlers, aged two and three. Life with three kids under 3.5 was hectic enough but on top of being a mum, I was also caring for a husband who was battling debilitating chronic back pain and unable to work. He could barely get out of bed, couldn't lift our children, couldn't even put on his own socks. To say it was tough is an understatement. Not surprisingly for someone in so much constant physical pain, my husband also developed depression. Mental illness and physical injury combined to create a very dark and difficult time – not just for him but for me too.

I was caring for four people who totally depended on me and was trying to hold it together myself. It was the most challenging time in my life and during this period, the communication skills I'd coasted through life with were put under extreme pressure.

Every conversation I had with my husband was fraught. He was in the depths of depression, defensive, detached, angry and quick to pick an argument. He became difficult to live with.

I was doing my best to love and support him but it was incredibly stressful. With three little kids in the house, it meant I had to initiate some very difficult conversations to work our way through this time. Suddenly, my natural, engrained skills on their own were not enough.

Despite having been a communications specialist for many years, I needed to do some self-development. I needed to turn to others for support and create strategies for communicating effectively with my husband during this time. I had to develop a growth mindset and stretch myself to learn new coping skills.

I needed to be on top of my game for our conversations if I wanted to have any chance of them connecting and going as well as they could. When you're under that much pressure, communication is incredibly difficult for both parties. Whether it's with a partner, family, friends or colleagues, when you're on edge and under intense stress, staying in control of your emotions and communicating at your best seems nearly impossible. But it can be done. My husband and I managed to get through the darkness of this time with our marriage intact. Had I not worked so intensely on managing myself and developing my communication skills, I'm not sure we would have.

The skills and strategies I drew on throughout 2014 changed everything for me – from my approach to communicating with my husband, to the way I dealt with difficult clients in my business and the way I related to my children when they pushed my buttons.

They're skills I still draw on heavily now and make a conscious decision to practice every day.

WE'RE PROGRAMMED TO WANT A QUICK FIX

The problem is, we often want an easy solution to our communication challenges, especially when we are under pressure. We want a few quick hacks that save the day and solve all our problems; a bandaid fix to get us through until things settle down and our existing communication skills are enough again. It's natural to want to avoid anything that requires too much effort if there's a shortcut we can take. After all, it works well for the credit industry, right? Why save for something, when you can buy it immediately with a credit card? That never ends badly...

Sadly, short-term communication solutions often achieve short-term results. You take a short course to learn skills that help you give and receive feedback or listen more actively. If it's a good course, you'll have every intention of putting it all into action. You may even improve some of your day-to-day interactions in the weeks afterwards. But many people walk out of such courses and continue communicating exactly as they've always done. Why? Because knowing and doing are two very different things.

The reality is you likely know the basics of good communication. You know how you should be communicating but you're not doing it. Or you're trying to do it, but it's not working, particularly when it really matters most: when the pressure is on. Whenever your emotions are running high, as are those of the people you're dealing with, you're at a loss. You remember the theory of how to communicate better (usually long after the moment you needed the skills). Or maybe you use some of the skills you've learnt when the going's good. It's when the going gets tough and the wheels fall off that you can't hold it together.

It's not that the skills you've developed or communication training you've done up until now are wrong. In fact, most communication courses (including the short ones) and books are jam-packed with valuable advice and practical tips. The problem is they don't focus on laying the foundations first. They jump straight to building the house before they've laid the slab, so to speak. They don't teach you about the preparatory work to manage yourself that must come first. And without that foundation, even the best communication skills won't work.

Most communication training is outward-focussed. You look at how you communicate with and manage *other* people. In this book, you will focus on yourself first. Effective communication starts with you and it's much more than being able to hold a conversation and listen half-decently. It's about choice, control, consideration, and courage. Then and only then, it is about communication.

Once you have these foundations which I'll discuss further in this book, you can implement the communication skills you already know to greater effect.

TECHNOLOGY, ENVIRONMENTAL AND SOCIAL DISRUPTION IS TURNING UP THE PRESSURE

All workplaces are in a time of disruptive change. Technology, regulations and expectations are changing at an incredible rate and our heads are spinning. Tasks are being outsourced and automated. People are uncertain about the future of their industries, the future of their roles and, in some cases, uncertain about whether their position will even exist tomorrow.

It's not surprising that we are stressed and struggling. Change is challenging, and uncertainty is unnerving. People respond emotionally, and reactions are heightened. The stress hormones

– adrenaline and cortisol – flood our bodies as the fight-or-flight response kicks in. There's an every-man-and-woman-for-themselves mentality because, under pressure, we tend to become more self-interested. It's a protection mechanism. People you've worked well with for years may turn on you or show an unexpected lack of respect for authority.

Around the world, in industries and professions of every sort, leaders like you are being thrust outside their comfort zone. You have to deliver unpopular messages and have tough conversations to manage your people through difficult times of mergers, redundancies, restructures, crises and emergencies. All the while, you must try to minimise the fallout and maintain a productive team. It's no wonder you're unsure about how to handle it.

Almost certainly, you're doing much more than you signed up for, and so feel ill-equipped to deal with it. Skills you've been building your whole life – the 'hard' technical skills that got you to where you are, that you have full confidence in – may have become useless and outdated.

Meanwhile, the soft skills – communication, relationship-building, leadership, adaptability, and emotional intelligence, which you may have dismissed as 'fluffy' extras for years – are now crucial for your success.

AVOIDANCE MAKES PROBLEMS GROW

Poor communication doesn't impact individuals alone; it impacts the success of businesses and organisations. Issues that start out as minor niggles and annoyances snowball into major conflict when leaders avoid talking about them. Unacceptable behaviour and poor performance is left unchecked because, rather than address the problems, leaders hope they'll disappear.

It's not surprising. Many of us were raised to try and keep the peace. Rather than address an issue head on, we think it's easier to find a work-around by giving the person a different task, switching them to another project, or adjusting office seating. Often, this is where the lack of formal communication training has an impact. We know how to communicate when times are easy, but when the pressure hits we flounder. We may have a couple of bad experiences communicating under pressure – an emotional blow-up or a sullen shutdown (from ourselves or our staff) – and we don't know what to do. So we do nothing.

Of course, avoidance doesn't make problems disappear. It makes them grow.

I was once brought into an organisation to coach a leader ahead of a conversation with a staff member accused of being aggressive by her colleagues. In my discussion with the leader, it emerged the aggressive behaviour and communication had been a problem for over a year. It had got to the point where other team members had approached the leader and said they would consider leaving the organisation if something wasn't done to address it directly.

I asked the leader what had been done up to that point. She looked at me blankly.

"Nothing," she replied, confused. "That's why you're here. To help me have that conversation."

I was surprised. This leader was a strong and capable woman yet had allowed this damaging behaviour to continue for over a year. Normally sensitive to her people, she had done nothing despite a significant impact on other staff members and the team's overall morale. Not a single conversation with the person involved.

"Why didn't you speak with them?" I asked, seeking to understand.

"I hoped it would get better on its own," she said.

In the years since, I've come across similar cases in many organisations. What could have been nipped in the bud early with a conversation about expected behaviour and perceptions had been left to become a major performance management and possible disciplinary issue because of communication avoidance.

The accused staff member had no idea her behaviour was perceived as aggressive by her colleagues. It wasn't her intention and she'd never received feedback until now. She was shocked when the conversation was eventually had; horrified and embarrassed to hear her colleagues thought poorly of her. Her intention was to be direct and assertive, but she had got it horribly wrong. Justifiably, one of the first questions she asked was, "Why has no-one told me this before?"

For her colleagues, the fallout of the delayed conversation was devastating too. They'd put up with the aggressive behaviour so long, it had impacted on their productivity and attitude toward work. Not only were staff angry at their aggressive colleague, they also felt let down by their leader and lost respect for her position.

YOU CAN'T BE A GREAT LEADER IF YOU'RE NOT A GREAT COMMUNICATOR

Here's the thing – you can't be a great leader without being a great communicator. It's as simple as that. You will never excel at leadership without this most important of soft skills, as the example above shows, no matter how intellectually intelligent, educated, or technically brilliant you are.

Leadership is about people. To be a leader in the true sense, people must want to follow you – even when times are tough. Especially when times are tough. To want to follow, people must feel a human connection with their leader. And to feel a human connection, there must be strong communication that motivates, encourages, inspires and empowers. You must also be able to regulate your emotions, have difficult conversations when required, and work with the emotions of others.

Good communication and leadership go hand-in-hand.

A leader in name isn't necessarily a leader in practice. A person who knows their job or industry backwards is not always a good leader of people. Nor is the person who can manage, coordinate, plan and organise well. Sure, this person may have people work for them who do what they are asked because of the leader's job title. But if people don't choose to follow a leader, they're not a *true* leader. As British wartime Prime Minister Winston Churchill is quoted as saying, "The difference between mere management and leadership is communication."

In my workshops, I ask participants to tell me about the best leaders they've ever worked for. They describe leaders who communicate clearly and calmly – even when under stress. People who are aware of their emotions and able to manage them. Leaders who are empathetic, assertive and articulate their vision, wants and needs in a respectful way so their team members know what's expected of them, where they're headed, why they're going there, what they need to do, and how they're tracking. Leaders who take personal responsibility for the way they communicate, regardless of what's going on around them.

On the flip side, participants describe the most ineffective and frustrating leaders as those who lack communication ability. They speak about leaders who deny their shortcomings, take credit for wins but blame staff for failures, justify poor behaviour and decisions, and get defensive when challenged. Leaders who lack self-awareness, don't take personal responsibility, are inconsistent, aggressive (or in some cases, passive), hold information to themselves, lack direction, can't make decisions or make decisions without consultation, give 'orders' with no explanation as to why, or don't communicate much at all.

It's not that they're incompetent – it's that they don't communicate effectively!

Some leaders tell me (defensively, of course) their 'like-it-or-lump-it' approach gets results, so they don't plan on changing. They argue that aggression is effective, and it doesn't matter whether people like them or not, as long as they get the job done.

To a degree they're right. You don't need everyone to be your best friend when you're in leadership. But what you do need is for people to respect you and ruling with intimidation, bullying, and aggression will not only not win you respect, but also put you at risk of breaking Federal anti-bullying laws.

Interestingly, the same lack of respect occurs if your communication style is passive as a leader. If you don't stand up for yourself and your team, if you can't communicate your message, be firm when required, influence outcomes and negotiate solutions, your staff won't respect you either. Again, they won't do their best for you. In fact, some (those with an aggressive or passive aggressive style) will make the most of the fact they can get away with poor behaviour without you pulling them into line.

Respect is everything as a leader. And to get it, you need to communicate in a way that connects.

LEARNING 'SOFT' SKILLS WILL TAKE YOU FURTHER

After many years skewed to a focus on hard skills, the value of soft skills like communication is finally starting to be recognised as workplaces wake up to the fact that a lack of basic communication and interpersonal skills amongst staff – particularly leaders – is holding them back.

This worldwide awakening, more than 80 years after publication of Dale Carnegie's game-changing book about the power of communication, *How to Win Friends and Influence People*, has led to many organisations overhauling their recruitment and hiring practices from a focus on technical skills to an emphasis on soft skills and values. Businesses look for the right person for the job, not simply the person with the right experience. Why? Because they've realised technical 'hard' skills are often easier to teach. From senior executive positions to entry-level administration jobs, more and more businesses are employing for soft skills and then teaching the technical job specific skills once the person starts.

Even tech giants like Google, which have traditionally focussed on hard STEM (science, technology, engineering and mathematics) skills are getting on board. In an article published on the *Washington Post* website on 20 December 2017, founding director of the Futures Initiative, Cathy N Davidson, explained how Google changed its approach to recruitment after 15 years of hiring on the strength of a person's STEM skills.

"In 2013, Google decided to test its hiring hypothesis by crunching every bit and byte of hiring, firing, and promotion data accumulated since the company's incorporation in 1998," Davidson explained.

"Project Oxygen shocked everyone by concluding that, among the eight most important qualities of Google's top employees, STEM expertise comes in dead last."

The seven top characteristics of success at Google, she said, are all soft skills:

▸ being a good coach
▸ communicating and listening well
▸ possessing insights into others (including different values and points of view)
▸ having empathy toward and being supportive of one's colleagues
▸ being a good critical thinker
▸ being a good problem solver
▸ being able to make connections across complex ideas

The Australian Antarctic Division cottoned on to the value of hiring for soft skills even earlier. In 2003, the youngest Chief Ranger at Parks Victoria, Rachael Robertson, 33, was reading the paper over breakfast when she came across a job advertisement that grabbed her attention. In her book, *Leading on the Edge* published in 2013, Robertson wrote: "The thing that caught my eye that morning was a photograph of penguins – in the careers section!" The ad was for the Australian Antarctic Division (AAD) and they were looking for an Expedition Station Leader. After the penguins, what intrigued Robertson was the way the job was advertised. Rather than seeking someone with the technical skills to lead a team in the harshest climate on Earth, the AAD was recruiting based on values, cultural fit and soft skills. Robertson decided to apply – not because she particularly wanted the job, but because she wanted to see firsthand how recruitment could be done this way, with the idea that she might get an interview and then take the learnings back to Parks Victoria.

One hundred and forty people applied for two station leader roles – one each at Davis Station and Mawson Station. After an initial phone interview, Robertson found she had been shortlisted to a top 14. Next came an array of medical tests, security checks, referee checks and a psychiatric test. Finally, two months later, came the last piece of the selection process – a week-long leadership 'boot camp' assessment in remote Tasmania. Over the course of the week, Robertson and the other applicants, who included a police commissioner, national distribution manager for Fairfax Media, CARE aid group leader, and others who had been to Antarctica before, were put through a wide range of 'games' aimed at testing their soft skills under pressure. Skills like communication, negotiation, empathy, problem-solving, and resilience, and values like respect and integrity. Robertson excelled, demonstrating through activities ranging from speeches and debates, to physical challenges, that she was a leader who could stay calm even when exhausted, communicate in a balanced and respectful way even when provoked, and was prepared to give early and fearless feedback to avoid minor issues developing into crisis (she decided to address an issue with a fellow applicant she felt disrespected her in a direct and private way).

Four weeks after the boot camp, Robertson received a call to say she'd got the job and would be the Expedition Leader of the year-long 58th Australian National Antarctic Research Expedition to Davis Station in 2005.

At 35, Robertson became the second female and the youngest expedition leader in AAD's history.

It didn't matter that she didn't know much about Antarctica, didn't ski, hated cold weather, and had been to the snow once on a Grade 6 excursion; once she was appointed, Robertson underwent a three-month intensive training program to learn the technical skills required to work and lead her team in the extreme conditions. The recruiters knew it would be easier to teach the technical side of surviving in Antarctica than to develop a person's soft skills. Having the best leader and communicator – someone who could be strong, but also show empathy – was the most important thing.

It's not senior leadership roles alone that are shifting to a focus on soft skills. When hiring a virtual assistant to join my own business team, I received an email from the agency that read, "We do not hire for skills or experience anymore as we have found in the past this has not been the most successful method. Instead, we hire for attitude, smarts, focus and work ethic and then we train them our way. In our experience, these candidates work out the best for us and our clients."

They hire for soft skills too! It seems there is a movement afoot. Not only will developing your soft skills increase your success in the workplace, it'll also increase your employability.

According to a report by Deloitte Access Economics titled 'Soft skills for business success' (May 2017), "soft skill-intensive occupations will account for two-thirds of all jobs [in Australia] by 2030, compared to half of all jobs in 2000". The report was prepared by Deloitte on behalf of DeakinCo. to assess the importance of obtaining and measuring soft skills to better understand areas that need to be improved in the Australian workforce and businesses. It found that: "Formal qualifications and technical skills are only part of the requirements for modern employees. 'Soft skills' and personal attributes are just as important to success."

In an article by Mark Eggleton published in the *Australian Financial Review* on 21 March 2018 titled 'Nothing soft about the key skills', LinkedIn managing director for Australia and New Zealand, Matt Tindale also highlighted the importance of soft skills. But he said the term soft skills annoyed him "because so-called soft skills are those that should be baked into every employee in the digital economy." Tindale said the term soft skills itself downplayed their importance because they are the skills you need to get jobs and promotions. Deloitte and Tindale are right: soft skills aren't lesser than hard skills – they're crucial for success.

OLD SCHOOL BEHAVIOUR LETS YOU (AND OTHERS) DOWN

Sadly, however, this change in focus from hard to soft skills is catching many people out. Highly experienced leaders are not getting jobs they thought they'd land. 'Next in line' no longer automatically determines who gets a promotion.

Yes, experience is important, but strong soft skills are right up there too. According to the Australian Institute of Management's 'Soft Skills Survey 2019', which studied the impact of soft skills on the future of Australian organisations, 80.5% of Australian business leaders think soft skills development is very or extremely important, and the top soft skill that Australian business leaders believe will be most crucial in 2019 is communication, attracting 75.6% of the vote. I think they're right.

The changing nature of workplace expectations and accepted behaviour means old-world practices don't fly anymore. The days of being able to yell and scream at people; of being able to threaten, intimidate and bully someone into good performance; or force them to toe the line through hierarchical power are over – or at the very least, dying fast.

This authoritarian approach – once considered acceptable – is now, in most cases, grounds for dismissal. That's not to say it doesn't happen. It does. There are pockets of industry and archaic workplace cultures that cling onto the past and still operate this way – just ask Lucas or our politicians in Canberra. But it's no longer the norm and workplaces are now looking for those who can lead assertively with compassion and manage their emotions while working with the emotions of others.

It's not just 'soft' customer, client or patient-based industries that are now valuing soft skills either. It's trades and digital-based workplaces too because people with these skills work well with others, stay calm under pressure, stand up for what's right, have difficult conversations when needed, build strong relationships and relate to people from all walks of life.

BUSTING THE TOP FIVE COMMUNICATION MYTHS

There are many myths and assumptions about effective communication and before we go any further, let me dispel the top five I come across through my work:

Myth 1: Communication ability is innate. You're either good at it or not.

Reality: Communication is a skill and like any skill it can be learned and developed, no matter what your starting point.

Myth 2: Communication is a soft 'fluffy extra'. It's nice but not essential to my success; my technical skills are more important.

Reality: Communication and human connection are key to personal and career success. It is as important as your technical skills. You don't have to be able to do the technical work if you can empower your team to do the technical work.

Myth 3: If I'm good at my job, or have been promoted to a leadership position, I must know how to communicate and therefore don't need to waste my time further developing these skills.

Reality: *No one* is a perfect communicator. Everyone can improve, even, and often especially senior executives. Many technically brilliant people are terrible communicators, as are many people promoted to leadership positions.

Myth 4: Other people need to communicate well with me in order for me to communicate well with them. If people didn't anger, frustrate or upset me, I'd be a good communicator.

Reality: Good communication isn't about other people, it's about you. It's an inside-out approach. Manage yourself and only then do you have a chance of managing – and connecting with – other people.

Myth 5: You have to be a certain type of person to communicate well (smart, educated, extroverted, confident).

Reality: Nope. Even nervous, uneducated introverts can communicate well if given the right foundations. Communication is about courage, not confidence.

Put simply, what you've been told up until now is wrong. Soft is the new hard.

In fact, soft isn't soft at all...

Chapter 3

INSIDE OUT

When I first started running workshops on effective communication, I made the same mistake as most communications courses and trainers: I focussed on teaching communication skills. I know what you're thinking – 'Um, Leah, isn't that kind of the point? It's a communication workshop after all'. But while my workshops were very well received and garnered excellent feedback, I quickly noticed something was missing.

My outward-looking approach that focussed on identifying communication styles and how to better communicate with other people wasn't leading to *permanent* change.

Participants left the sessions with a whole swag of new skills and ideas for having difficult conversations but only some implemented them. And, of those, most only changed the way they communicated in the short term immediately following the workshop before reverting to what they'd always done. How did I know this? Because these same people would contact me a few weeks afterward asking for tips to help them have their next difficult conversation, even though they'd been taught the skills already. Their old habits quickly resurfaced. It shouldn't have been surprising because when under pressure, we stick to what we know and the communication style we're most comfortable with – even when it's not the best approach.

That wasn't what I wanted.

I wasn't interested in my workshops being a short-term quick fix that was ultimately ineffective, like the diet shakes that help you lose weight, only to have you put every kilogram back on the minute you go back to eating normal food. The purpose of my workshops was to teach and empower people to make lasting changes to the way they communicate. Changes that not only improve the outcomes of their conversations but improve success in all aspects of their life – personal and professional.

I started asking myself why. Why, when people knew how to communicate more effectively after attending my workshop – or any communications training course for that matter – couldn't they do it? It's the same as asking why, when we know what to eat to lose weight, do we still reach for the chocolate cake?

I learned to identify those who would struggle to implement the skills they'd learnt even before they'd left my workshops. They were the 'yeah, but' people. The people who'd come up to me at the end and say, "That was great, but I have an aggressive boss who yells at me, so I can't have that conversation", or "Yeah, but that person is mean to me or wronged me in the past, so why should I be respectful and calm with them?"

My answer was always the same, delivered with compassion and empathy, but also honesty: it's not about the other person, it's about you. It's about *you* taking personal responsibility and communicating in the best way you can, regardless of what the other person is doing. Success is being able to walk away at the end, comfortable that you did everything in your power to communicate in the best way possible for the situation. You may not get the outcome you want but you know you did all you could.

Some people took this final advice well, while others immediately became defensive. "But that's not fair!" they'd exclaim. "I know," I'd reply gently. "But life's not fair sometimes."

It was after delivering my workshop to staff at a retail business, where team morale was terrible and accusations of intimidation and aggression rife, that I realised I'd been missing a key ingredient in my teaching. I was skipping to the end of the communication process – the conversation – without first laying the foundations that underpinned it. I was providing a quick fix in terms of communication tips, without the most important part: helping people to first manage themselves so they could break old communication habits and take control – even when under intense pressure.

So, I started thinking and reading classics in the field, such as Stephen Covey's *The 7 Habits of Highly Effective People* published in 1989, Viktor Frankl's *Man's Search for Meaning* from 1946, Daniel Goleman's *Emotional Intelligence* from 1995, and Dale Carnegie's *How to Win Friends and Influence People*, 1936.

I read a few modern-day bestsellers too like Mark Manson's *The Subtle Art of Not Giving a F*ck* from 2016, Sheryl Sandberg's *Lean In* published in 2013, and Jamila Rizvi's *Not Just Lucky*, 2017. These books are not communication books. Yet the foundations that underpin our ability to communicate effectively lie at their core.

I also reflected on my own life and the strategies that helped me communicate with my husband throughout 2014.

As Stephen Covey said in *The 7 Habits of Highly Effective People*, if you want to improve your communication, you need to start from the inside out. What I needed to do was start with the individual and work outwards from there; with self-management the first port of call, and communication with others the last. I needed to teach people how to do the thinking first, before they said a word. I needed to show them how working on their mind and thought processes would help them work better with others. That is how this book was born.

IT STARTS WITH MINDSET

Your ability to communicate effectively will be helped or hindered by your mindset. Helped, if you approach communication from a growth mindset; hindered, if you come at it with a fixed mindset. Let me explain.

A fixed mindset is the belief that you are who you are and you can't change. It's a 'bad-luck-this-is-who-I-am' mentality. You see your intelligence and behaviour as fixed – you believe you're either good at something or you're not, and your abilities are unchanging. You see your potential as predetermined and don't like to be challenged. You prefer to hide your weaknesses than admit them and work to overcome them.

If you come at this book with a fixed mindset, you will struggle to put the skills and steps into practice.

To be able to put the strategies outlined in this book into effect, it needs to be approached with a growth mindset. According to psychologist and author of *Mindset: Changing the way you think to fulfil your potential* (2012), Dr Carol Dweck, a growth mindset is based on the belief that "everyone can change and grow through application and experience".

You must believe you can learn new ways of doing things and be willing to do the work to get there. You must believe you can train your brain to approach challenges in a new way.

Shifting from a fixed to a growth mindset isn't easy, but it is possible. As Canadian doctor, psychiatrist, psychoanalyst and university researcher Dr Norman Doidge explains in his book *The Brain That Changes Itself* (2007), our brains can rewire themselves. Scientists used to think that our brains were pretty much wired for life by the time we reached young adulthood. Doige disproved that theory. His research shows that, thanks to a process called neuroplasticity, we can create new nerve pathways and neural connections. Our brains can adapt and change with practice and concerted effort, and it starts when we regularly put ourselves out of our comfort zone. That's what I'm asking you to do right now.

IMPROVING YOUR COMMUNICATION SKILLS IS AN 'INSIDE JOB'

To communicate effectively with other people, you've got to prepare yourself for effective communication by working on how you manage yourself first. Improving your communication skills is what I call an 'inside job'. By this, I mean that you have to change from the inside out.

That realisation prompted me to change my workshops by adding mindset and emotional intelligence learning into the sessions. I began to explain the role that personal responsibility and choice play in our ability to respond to other people effectively, regardless of situation and circumstance. I showed leaders that there is no one *right* communication style at all times; consideration is the key. I dismissed the idea that confidence was essential and focussed on courage instead, because even when you're not feeling confident, you can still be brave and decide to speak up.

The results were immediate and the response from participants incredible. Those who did the work and implemented these strategies that laid the foundations – who focussed hard on making real change to themselves first – saw how putting in the effort *before* they communicated led to long-lasting and significant results. They could see a clear path forward and even if they looked at it with trepidation, they could clearly see the steps they needed to take to get to where they wanted to go with their communication.

This book is about those steps.

Like my workshops, these steps are not a quick-fix Band-Aid approach or a bag of tricks. All that does is set you up for failure; it makes you more despondent when you can't put your newly learnt communication skills into practice. These are steps to make permanent change. They are foundations that underpin the way you communicate with and relate to other people. If you put them into practice, if you do not pay them lip service but truly embrace them and live them, your communication will undoubtedly improve – even when under the most intense pressure.

That feeling of being at the mercy of others, of being a victim to a situation, circumstance and your emotions will be gone. You won't just improve your communication, you'll change your entire approach to life and with that, you'll increase your success exponentially. Not just the outcomes of your conversations but your success in all relationships, and your health and well-being too.

Am I overstating it? No. What you will learn in the next six chapters is that important. In fact, I'm going to go right out there and say it can and will change your life.

Just like it did mine.

Chapter 4

KNOW YOUR COMMUNICATION STYLE

Before we look at laying the foundations to improve your communication, let's look at where your communication style currently sits and how it might be helping or hindering your success. What are your defaults? By the end of this book, you'll be able to control your defaults, so don't worry if your current default communication style falls short of where you'd like, especially when you are under pressure.

Simply ask yourself the questions on the following pages and analyse which style you answer 'yes' more than 'no' to. Don't think too much. Don't labour over these questions. Answer them honestly and dispassionately. Like any process of change, it will help if you understand where you are today, before you make any changes, and ensure you get more out of the strategies further along in this book.

THE FOUR COMMON 'GO-TO' COMMUNICATION STYLES: WHICH IS YOURS?

How we communicate in any given circumstance will often depend on a wide range of factors: How we're feeling at the time, our emotional health, the situation or circumstance, our relationship with the person we're communicating with, and the other person's personality and communication style.

Of the four styles outlined below – aggressive, passive, passive-aggressive and assertive – most of us will use them all at different times. That's totally normal.

Yet despite the many variables, most of us have a go-to communication style, a style we revert to, particularly at times of stress. For me, my go-to style in the workplace is assertive. I stay calm under pressure, ask for what I want and need, and have difficult conversations with empathy and respect. However, I can sometimes fall into passive and say yes when I should say no because I genuinely want to help and please people; and I can also be unintentionally aggressive when my passion and drive for fast action overwhelms others.

It's your go-to style that I want you to discover and then reflect on as you read this book.

Because our focus is communicating in the workplace, I want you to wear your work 'hat' when you answer the questions on the following pages. Why do I make that distinction? Because while some people communicate similarly at work and at home, other people's styles are poles apart depending on their environment. For these people, answering the questions with a whole-of-life hat on will skew the results. So let's focus on how you communicate at work.

You also need to be honest with yourself. We all get good at telling ourselves stories and making excuses to justify our behaviour. That won't help you here. If you truly want to improve your communication, you need to stop bullshitting yourself.

Righto, here goes...

AGGRESSIVE (I WIN, YOU LOSE)

Do you find yourself doing, saying or behaving in any of the following ways? Remember, you might be surprised to recognise yourself in some of these statements, so be aware that this book is about helping you to make changes if needed, not about criticising or punishing. Do you:

	YES	NO
Love to win arguments and score points.		
Disregard other people's feelings, opinions and needs (intentionally or unintentionally).		
Get annoyed when other people discuss their feelings.		
Focus on action without considering others because you 'just need to get the job done'.		
Need to be right, or feel that you are usually right (and others are wrong).		
Like to have the last word in an argument or discussion.		
See things in black and white – with little room for grey in the middle.		
Make conversations about you.		
Raise your voice, shout, or talk over others when frustrated or to convey an important point.		
Not listen to other people, or listen to respond rather than to hear.		
Interrupt when others are talking.		
Act defensively and blame others for mistakes, problems and failures, rather than take personal responsibility.		
Communicate bluntly, with no filter, or with inappropriate honesty (such as telling someone their child's name is horrendous).		

Have unrealistically high expectations of others.

Focus on negatives and problems, rather than solutions and opportunities.

Not care what other people think of your communication style and take a 'like it or lump it' approach

Threaten, bully and/or intimidate people into following your instructions because nothing else you've tried has worked.

TOTAL YES = _____   TOTAL NO = _____

If you answered yes to more questions than no, your go-to style may be aggressive.

The problem with aggressive:

▸ People do what you want, but no more than that. You lose that most precious of qualities: discretionary effort. When you communicate aggressively, people act out of fear and obligation. They feel they have no choice but to obey, and that is an uncomfortable feeling. Most people will resent you for making them feel they lack any power or choice. You may get what you want day-to-day, but the minute you need help that's a bit above and beyond, no-one is around. All you'll hear are crickets chirping.

▸ People lose respect for you. A common catch-cry from aggressive communicators, particularly in the workplace, is: "It doesn't matter whether people like me, as long as I get results." While it might not matter whether people like you, it certainly does matter if they don't respect you. Aggressive communication makes people feel worthless. When you resort to power, position, privilege, or intimidation to get your way, you undermine people's respect for you. They will stop wanting to help you, and may even undermine you behind your back. You stop getting the best out of people if you don't have their respect. This not only impacts them, it impacts you and your success too.

KNOW YOUR COMMUNICATION STYLE   **37**

- You will make mistakes. If the only opinion or point of view you listen to is your own – because people are too afraid of you to voice their opinions, ideas and questions – you will make mistakes. There will be something you haven't considered, or a blind spot you're not aware of. Eventually you'll miss something. No-one respects you enough to try to protect you from it; they many even hope you fail to bring you down a peg or two. It may only be something minor, or it may be major. Whatever it is, it is something that could have been avoided if only you'd listened and sought input and feedback.

- Your behaviour distracts and detracts from your message. We've all been there. Either on the giving or receiving end. When we (or someone else) have totally lost our cool, the focus becomes our poor behaviour, regardless of how legitimate our message is. The conflict stops being about the issue, and becomes about the yelling and the anger. Instead of listening, people tune out or tell you to calm down (which never works!) and what you're saying becomes irrelevant compared to how you're saying it. In short, your communication becomes totally ineffective.

All that said, aggressive communication does have its place. There are times when it's entirely appropriate. Such times include:

- if your rights or safety are threatened
- you need someone to stop or take action immediately
- someone is about to get hurt.

The problem arises when you rely on or default to aggression under pressure.

PASSIVE (I LOSE, YOU WIN)

Do you find yourself doing, saying or behaving in any of the following ways? Do you:

YES   NO

Not speak up for yourself or express your beliefs, even when you want to.

Avoid conflict and confrontation, even if someone is treating you badly.

Avoid giving negative feedback and having difficult conversations.

Try to please other people and say 'yes' when you want to say 'no'.

Appear overly easy-going by agreeing with others constantly, rather than contributing your own opinions or thoughts.

Apologise unnecessarily (constantly saying 'sorry') or use the word 'just' a lot – "Just a quick email" or "Just checking if you've had a chance to read that report yet."

Put your own needs last.

Talk yourself down (before someone else can) and dismiss your success as 'luck'.

Find eye-contact uncomfortable.

Not contribute in meetings unless asked directly.

Dismiss compliments and positive feedback.

TOTAL YES = _____   TOTAL NO = _____

If you answered yes to more questions than no, your go-to style may be passive.

While there are times when passive communication is appropriate, if it's your default position it will hold you back and limit your success.

The problem with passive:

- If you don't speak up for yourself, others can (and will!) walk all over you.

- People will disregard your opinions and needs – sometimes intentionally because they know they can and you won't say anything, but sometimes unintentionally because they don't know your thoughts and feelings.

- You'll be passed over for jobs and promotions if you don't contribute or share your ideas and initiatives.

- You become complicit in poor choices – if a decision is made and you don't speak up against it, your silence will be taken as compliance.

- You expect other people to be mind readers. You think: 'They should know why I'm upset', rather than have a conversation.

- You will experience feelings of stress, seething anger and resentment because you feel like you're being walked over.

- You may find you have explosions of aggressive communication. Passive communicators often communicate in extremes. They keep their feelings bottled up until their anger builds to a point when they can't hold it in any longer and then they explode, often spectacularly.

Like aggressive communication, passive does have its place though. Circumstances when passive might be the best communication choice include:

- when trying to balance out a relationship and allow another person to shine or make a decision. (Compromise is essential in any relationship.)

- when dealing with a manipulative person who is provoking you for a reaction.

- when being assertive would hurt the other person and not benefit you.

- when you don't have the experience or skills needed to answer a question. (Sometimes it's more appropriate to let others take the lead.)

PASSIVE-AGGRESSIVE (LOSE-LOSE)

Do you find yourself doing, saying or behaving in any of the following ways? Do you:

YES   NO

Express your anger and unhappiness indirectly through your actions, attitude, body language, tone and behaviour.

Deny you're angry, even when you are. You may hear yourself making comments such as, "I'm fine", "I'm not angry; why would I be angry?"

Dismiss or deflect emotionally direct (honest) communication or efforts by others to find out how you feel. You might respond by saying: "Whatever", "Fine", "If you think there's a problem, that's your problem."

Use sarcasm or an excessively pleasant voice to disguise anger or an aggressive overtone. "Nooooooo, why would I be angry?" or "I said it with a smile so of course I'm genuine", or "I'm only joking. Can't you take a joke?"

Criticise people behind their backs, but feel unable to raise issues directly with them.

Play little 'jokes' that undermine others to 'get back' at them, such as not telling someone the meeting time changed, knowing they would then miss attending.

Use 'the silent treatment' with people when you're unhappy about something. For example, if someone upsets you, you don't speak to them for the rest of the day.

Give backhanded compliments, like: "That's a lovely dress for one you bought at K-Mart".

Deliberately perform a work task badly because you didn't want to do it in the first place.

Make vague comments and criticisms rather than have a direct conversation with the person in question.

TOTAL YES = _____   TOTAL NO = _____

If you answered yes to more questions than no, your go-to style may be passive-aggressive.

Passive-aggressive communication is my favourite to talk about because I'm on a mission to stamp it out of existence! It's my least favourite to encounter in real life due to its manipulative and damaging impact – although it is rife in workplaces and personal relationships.

Of the four styles, it is the only one I believe does not have any place in either our workplaces or our personal lives.

The problem with passive-aggressive:

▸ Passive-aggressive is a lose-lose style of communication: You won't get your needs met because you don't ask for what you want and need, and the other person can't fix the problem because they don't know what the problem is!

▸ Passive-aggressive communication is manipulative, immature, infuriating and destructive. We're all guilty of it at times as it's easy to fall into, but if you find yourself communicating in this way I urge you to work hard to stop!

▸ It undercuts trust and respect as people know you're not telling them how you really feel. People may cut you out of conversations and decision-making as they don't trust you to be honest.

▸ It makes it difficult for you to get your goals met, lets minor problems escalate into major conflicts and, in extreme cases (such as when you deliberately don't speak to a colleague for weeks), can be a form of emotional abuse.

ASSERTIVE (I WIN, YOU WIN)

Do you find yourself doing, saying or behaving in any of the following ways? Do you:

YES   NO

Stand up for yourself and your point of view, while respecting the opinions, rights and beliefs of others.

State your point clearly, firmly and directly – but respectfully.

Treat all people – whether they're the CEO or cleaner – with the same level of respect.

Ask for what you want and need.

Accept and respect that no-one else thinks like you and that different opinions are OK.

Communicate calmly and evenly, even under pressure.

Take a problem-solving approach to conflict by offering alternatives and solutions. You try to find win-win outcomes, in which everyone feels they achieved their desired outcome.

Have conversations about behaviours or comments that have upset you, even when they're uncomfortable and before they develop into major conflict.

Avoid vague communication and over-explaining.

Behave and communicate in a consistent way, regardless of what's going on in your personal or work life, so that people know what they're going to get when they speak to you.

Put yourself in other people's shoes and communicate empathetically.

Be appropriately honest.

Say no with confidence.

Ask for help when you need it.

Know your message and stick to it.

Consider other people's opinions.

Know when to speak up and also when to stand down.

Negotiate, compromise and concede when required.

TOTAL YES = _____   TOTAL NO = _____

If you answered yes to more questions than no, your go-to style may be assertive.

The framework and model outlined in this book is strongly geared towards increasing your assertiveness. In my experience, it is the most effective style for most high-pressure communication (and communication in general). By following the steps outlined in the following chapters, you will develop your assertive communication skills and be more successful in your conversations.

The benefits of assertive:

- ► Your needs are met and you endeavour to ensure the other person's needs are met too.
- ► It gets results because you put forward your point and ask for what you want and need.
- ► It creates honest relationships because people know where you stand.
- ► People are less likely to take advantage of you.
- ► It earns respect and increases recognition.
- ► You'll have disagreements rather than arguments.
- ► It reduces stress because you have conversations early, rather than let tension build.
- ► You don't feel threatened and victimised because you stand up for yourself.
- ► It allows you to be heard. Being assertive won't always get you the outcome you want, but sometimes covering your butt is the only option left and having your opinion tabled will help you do that.

The downside of assertive:

Although it is a win-win style of communication and the most appropriate style to use when communicating under pressure in most circumstances, there is a downside to assertiveness.

- Some people won't like you standing up for yourself, particularly if that is new behaviour for you and they're used to pushing you around.

- Some may mistake your assertiveness for aggression, particularly very passive communicators who struggle with any direct communication – even when you are fair and respectful.

- Being assertive can be uncomfortable. Standing up for yourself can be nerve wracking and downright scary sometimes.

- It's not always the best approach. There are times when a passive or aggressive approach are the most appropriate (see Chapter 7 for more information on how to consider the best approach depending on the circumstances).

FROM KNOWLEDGE TO ACTION

We've covered a lot of ground in these first four chapters. Now you understand:

- your own communication style

- what a people problem looks like

- why your communications skills may be buckling under pressure, and

- why soft skills are becoming the focus worldwide and will advance your career.

So, it's time to get down to business: how to improve your communication with practical tips and strategies. To do that, you need to turn this knowledge into action. Knowledge of the problems alone is not enough to help solve your communication problems. So I'm going to introduce you to an action plan. It is a five-step sequential model of the building blocks that underpin effective communication. A model I call The Five Cs.

THE FIVE Cs OF EFFECTIVE COMMUNICATION

CHOICE › CONTROL › CONSIDERATION › COURAGE › COMMUNICATION

Figure 1: The Five Cs of Effective Communication

Source: Mether, Leah (2019) *Soft is the New Hard: How to Communicate Under Pressure*

The Five C model is a series of steps developed as a result of my experience at a time when I was under intense pressure and my resilience was tested (see My Story in Chapter 2). It's informed by the thinking of the authors I've referred to in the early chapters of this book: Dale Carnegie, Victor Frankl, Stephen Covey and Daniel Goleman and I know it works because I've lived and practiced it now for years, and so have my many corporate clients.

It's the model this book is based on.

The model is simple, but don't confuse simple with easy: living this model will be one of the most difficult challenges you'll face in your entire life. But it's a game changer.

The Five Cs provide you with the steps to follow in both the lead up to and delivery of your communication. If you follow this model, you'll be able to communicate in a way that advances your career and improves your personal and professional relationships. It will not only give you a clear structure you can follow for every interaction and communication for the rest of your life, it will also help you improve your mindset, build resilience, control your emotions, enable you to respond consistently and calmly, and give you the best chance of getting the result you want.

These five steps now form the basis for all communication in my life.

The first thing most people notice about this model is that communication – the bit they are most focussed on – is at the end. It's often remarked on with surprise but its positioning is absolutely appropriate. The last of the five steps to effective communication is applying communication skills. It's not the starting point.

You must do the thinking first. That reflection is found in the four foundational steps. This model addresses how to get those foundations in place. Yet most of us are trained to start with communication. No wonder we fail and slip back into old habits quickly – because we haven't been shown how to do the groundwork.

In fact, every step in this model – choice, control, consideration, courage and communication – is deliberately placed in its position. Each step builds on the one before it and with each step you take you'll improve your communication.

But let me assure you that you do not need to complete all five steps before you start seeing benefits. From the very first moment on this journey, your life will begin to change in startling and exciting ways.

IT STARTS WITH CHOICE

When my husband's health was at its worst, as I described in Chapter 2, I had to make a choice about my own personal character, regardless of his response to me. I needed to be in control of my emotions. I had to be considerate of him and crystal clear about what I wanted to say to him (my message) and how to best say it. And, finally, I had to be courageous enough to raise the subject in the first place, and then committed to follow through with the conversation.

Here is a summary of each step in the model:

Choice

Effective communication is underpinned by the choice to take personal responsibility for your communication and behaviour. A choice to live from a growth – rather than fixed or victim – mindset. A choice about how you respond in any situation, no matter how difficult the circumstance or what the other person is doing or saying. A choice over your character as a human being. And let me say it again because it is my most important message to you in this book: a choice to take personal responsibility for your communication.

Control

Once you've made the choice about how you want to live your life, the next step is control. Control is not about turning everyone into robots who don't show emotion; it's about developing emotional intelligence so you are able to regulate your response. It's grounded in strong self-awareness and an understanding of how to manage yourself in the moment, even when that moment is full of intense pressure and stress. However, control isn't only about being in charge of what you say and do, it's also about knowing what to let go of; about understanding what's out of your control and therefore not something you should invest your time and energy into thinking about.

Consideration

When you have choice and control nailed down, we'll move onto consideration. There is no one right or wrong way to communicate, which is why consideration is key. You need to consider your response based on the situation, circumstance and who you're dealing with. You need to consider where the other person is coming from and what is likely to best connect with them in order to get the outcome you want. It's not all about you and what you want to say.

Courage

After consideration comes courage. The idea that courage trumps confidence came from an unlikely source: former Australian politician from the obscure Australian Motoring Enthusiast Party, Ricky Muir, who was elected as a Senator for Victoria in the 2013 Federal Election on the back of preference deals, despite winning a record-low primary vote of just 0.51%. Muir was addressing leaders at the 2017 Gippsland Community Leadership Program residential in Inverloch when he uttered these powerful words: "It's about courage, not confidence". While Muir was referring to politics, his words are just as applicable to communication. You don't need to be an extrovert to communicate effectively. What you do need to be is brave enough to overcome your self-doubt and fear of failure, and courageous enough to stand up for what you believe in, even when it scares you.

Communication

Only after you've completed these four Cs are you ready to communicate – once the foundations are in place. And this is where the specific skills – the tips and tricks you usually get served up at communication courses – finally come in. It's time to do the work, by which I mean, act on the knowledge you gain. It's no good knowing communication skills if you don't implement them. In the communication chapter we'll discuss how you put your communication skills into real-life practice in an effective way.

ROME WASN'T BUILT IN A DAY

I've filled this book with the most valuable information I know so you've got a whole arsenal at your disposal. I want you to have a resource you can turn to whenever the pressure is on. But the risk of having so much advice in one book is overwhelm: there's only so much you can take in.

So don't expect to be able to put all the ideas into action after the first pass. You don't need to do it all at once; small changes will have a big impact. Shifting your mindset from fixed to growth will, on its own, transform your communication. Remember, this book is about helping you deal with pressure, not putting you under more of it. Cut yourself some slack. Pick one or two points from each chapter to start with and build from there. Any movement forward is a step in the right direction.

GAME ON

Now, roll up your sleeves and get ready to dive in. Soft is the new hard but I'm going to show you a framework that will make it a whole lot easier.

Chapter 5

CHOICE

Forget other people. It doesn't matter if Bill's being an asshole, Sharon's giving you the passive-aggressive silent treatment, or John's work isn't up to scratch. It doesn't matter what other people do or how they respond. No matter what happens, you have a choice about the sort of communicator you want to be.

It's not about other people; it's about you.

If you want to improve your success at work and in your personal relationships, the single most important thing you can do is take personal responsibility for your communication and behaviour. I'm talking about extreme responsibility, with no room for 'yeah, but...'

Of course, as I have mentioned before, it's easier to blame other people for 'making' you communicate a certain way – that's why most people do it. But remember that no matter how others communicate with you or what the situation or circumstance, *you* have the power to choose your response and behaviour. You get to choose how someone or something impacts you. It's time to reclaim your power and get conscious about the choices you make. Why? Because if you don't make a choice to take personal responsibility for your communication, you'll never be able to communicate consistently and effectively. You'll never be able to implement the fifth of the five Cs if your response is dependent on how other people behave.

Choice is why other communications training you've done may not have worked. Choice is why you're in this predicament. And choice is what's going to set you free.

"Yeah, but Leah, you haven't been through what I've been through. You haven't faced the pressure I've faced. You haven't worked for a boss like I have. You haven't been in charge of a team like my team. You haven't experienced the grief, tragedy, devastation and challenges I have." No. I haven't. But your circumstances need not determine your choices. Your power to choose transcends even the toughest of circumstances. And if you don't believe me, believe Viktor Frankl.

A MAN'S SEARCH FOR MEANING

Viktor Frankl was an Austrian neurologist and psychiatrist, born in 1905. He was married, had a loving family and he was Jewish. During World War II, Frankl spent three years imprisoned in Nazi ghettos and various concentration camps, including the infamous Auschwitz.

Forced to work as a slave labourer in the depths of winter, starved and witness to some of the most horrific atrocities in human history, Frankl captured his experiences in a book published shortly after the war that was eventually translated as *Man's Search for Meaning* (1946), which went on to sell more than 10 million copies worldwide.

Despite what he lived through, and the fact his wife, father, mother and brother all perished under Nazi rule, Frankl found meaning in his captivity and wrote this of his experience:

"In the concentration camps…we watched and witnessed some of our comrades behave like swine while others behaved like saints. Man has both potentialities within himself; which one is actualised depends on decisions but not on conditions."

Amidst the horror of war, Frankl discovered that, even in the most brutal of circumstances, we all have the power to choose. No matter what. No matter how bad it gets, we always have a choice.

Here's what he wrote: "Everything can be taken from a man but one thing: the last of the human freedoms—to choose one's attitude in any given set of circumstances, to choose one's own way. When we are no longer able to change a situation, we are challenged to change ourselves. Between stimulus and response there is a space. In that space is our power to choose our response. In our response lies our growth and our freedom."

Let those words sink in. Go back and read over them again. Type them up and print them out. Stick them on the wall behind your desk, just like I have. Better yet, if you've never read *Man's Search for Meaning*, go and buy a copy or borrow one from your local library.

Here is a man who had every reason to rail against the injustice of the world and respond with vitriol, hate, aggression, hopelessness and despair in the face of what he had experienced. Yet Frankl realised that no matter what happened – even when living in a human hell – he had the power to choose his response. In fact, in the end, he says it was the only thing he did have. Wow.

Now, I'm not saying you haven't been through a lot in your life. I'm not saying you haven't experienced tragedy, hardship, injustice or incredible challenges. I get that those experiences have an impact on who you are and what you do. In fact, they can cause incredible grief, sorrow and anger and it's important to let yourself feel those emotions and work through them. But you are not at the mercy of those sorrows forever. If Viktor Frankl can exercise his power to choose in the midst of the Holocaust, you can too.

It has been more than 70 years since Frankl first published his experiences from the war and his words stand the test of time. *Man's Search for Meaning* is still often credited as the catalyst for people changing their life. Authors from Steven Covey (*The 7 Habits of Highly Effective People*) to Mark Manson (in *The Subtle Art of Not Giving a F*ck*) reference his work on the power of choice.

I am doing the same here with a focus on communication. Only you get to choose how you communicate. You choose how you respond to those around you. You choose the sort of leader you want to be.

IT'S EASIER TO BLAME OTHER PEOPLE

Deny. Blame. Justify. Defend. These are four of the most common automatic emotion-charged responses when we're forced to communicate under pressure. We don't even think about our reaction, we just 'do', with no conscious awareness.

We yell at our kids in frustration. We get defensive when given feedback without really listening to what's being said. We blame others for stirring us up and 'making' us explode in anger. And we sometimes justify it all with statements like 'it's ok, because that's the culture of our company'.

Over and over again in our lives, we give up the power of our own choice and instead fall into default behaviour that works against us. We blow up in anger at our team and lose their respect. We don't listen to constructive feedback and then make the very mistake we were warned about. We don't address the poor behaviour of our colleagues and then wonder why they continue with that behaviour.

The reality is, it is always tempting to blame other people. That way we don't have to ask the hard questions of ourselves and our behaviours. That way we don't have to own our own failings and weaknesses, or admit we got it wrong.

Consider your response when you're cut off by another car in traffic: Do you react automatically, swearing, tooting the horn, or flashing your headlights without thought or control? Or, in the moment, are you able to take a deep breath and retain your composure?

Ask yourself the same question about the way you respond when something unexpected, frustrating or negative happens in the workplace or your personal relationships. Do you take control of your response? Do you remember that you have a choice, or do you forget about your ability to choose in the heat of the moment?

THE LINE OF CHOICE

In my workshops, I use a deceptively simple, but oh-so-effective above/below the line model adapted from Global Leadership Foundation to highlight the difference conscious choice can make to the way you lead, behave and communicate. Co-founded by Gayle Hardie and Malcolm Lazenby in 2003, Global Leadership Foundation is an Australian-based company intent on raising the emotional health levels across the world by developing, strengthening and transforming people's leadership potential. They adapted their use of the model from American businessman and author Robert Kiyosaki.

First, I ask participants to tell me about the communication behaviours of the worst or most difficult people they've ever worked with. Very quickly we fill the lower half of a whiteboard with words and statements like aggressive, dishonest, blame, take credit, don't apologise, think they're always right, don't explain, inconsistent, play favourites, toxic, manipulative, don't communicate – the list goes on.

I then ask participants to tell me about the best people to work with. How do they communicate and behave? We fill the top half of the board with words and statements like honest, calm, consistent, respectful, measured, clear, fair, and owns mistakes.

Once we have our two lists, I draw a line between the two, separating the top positive qualities, from the bottom negative ones. Then I give the line a name – the line of choice.

People who operate above the line take personal responsibility for their communication and behaviour. They make a choice about how they respond. People who operate below the line don't think, they just react. They respond emotionally in the moment without any conscious thought, choice or control. They don't make use of what American psychotherapist and author, Tara Bennett-Goleman, refers to as 'the magic quarter second' in her 2001 book *Emotional Alchemy: How Your Mind Can Heal Your Heart*. The tiny space in time between impulse and action, when a thought can be 'caught' before it turns into an emotional reaction.

The above-and-below-the-line model resonates. I've seen teams use it to develop a shared language to call out poor behaviour in a non-confrontational way. "Mate, that's a bit below the line. How can we get back up above it?" someone might say to a colleague who has reacted angrily (and automatically) to bad news about a sale falling through.

I've also seen people use it as a way of venting in a compartmentalised manner. They've walked into a team meeting and announced, "I just need to go below the line for a second" – had their moment – and then been able to move on by stating "Ok, now let me get back above the line", consciously choosing to move on.

Try it yourself. Divide a page into two with a line through the middle labelled the line of choice. In the top half write the words 'personal responsibility' and in the bottom write 'deny, blame, justify, defend'. Stick it somewhere you can see it as a physical reminder to make choice part of your consciousness.

Figure 2: The Line of choice

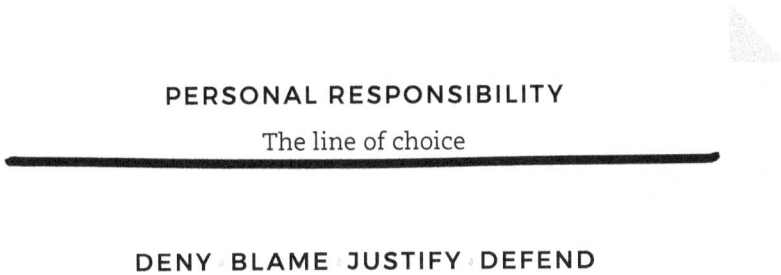

PERSONAL RESPONSIBILITY

The line of choice

DENY BLAME JUSTIFY DEFEND

Source: Global Leadership Foundation

A TALE OF TWO TRIANGLES

Building on the above-and-below-the-line model, you also have a choice about what type of person you want to be – a victim of circumstance or the creator of your life. You might be thinking, 'Jeez Leah, that's a bit deep. What the hell does it have to do with communication?' The short answer? Everything.

Your mindset and the choices you make about how you face the world underpin your ability to communicate effectively. It is highlighted beautifully by comparing two models of mindset – Stephen Karpman's 'Karpman Drama Triangle' (1968) and David Emerald's 'The Empowerment Dynamic' (2005).

As you read about each model on the following pages, consider which one you inhabit most.

Karpman, a psychologist, first presented his model in an article titled *Fairy Tales and Script Drama Analysis* in 1968. He won the Eric Berne Memorial Scientific Award in 1972 for the article, in which he used an inverted triangle to represent three positions – victim, persecutor and rescuer.

Figure 3: The Karpman Drama Triangle

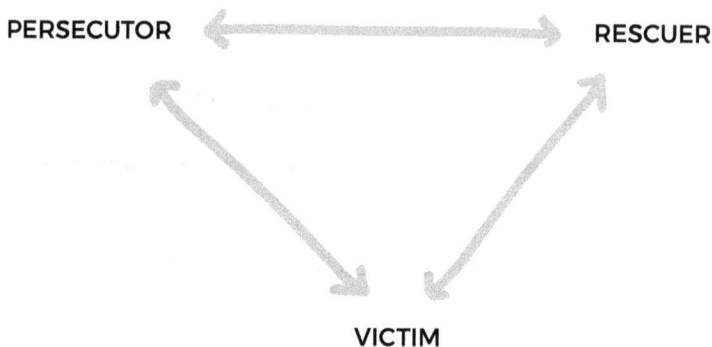

PERSECUTOR ←-------------------→ RESCUER

VICTIM

Source: Karpman, Stephen (1968) *Fairy Tales and Script Drama Analysis*

THE VICTIM PERSPECTIVE

According to Karpman, a victim is someone who focuses on the problems in their life and the events they don't want to happen. They're driven by thoughts like 'poor me', 'life's not fair' and 'why do bad things always happen to me?' Similar to those who operate below the line, they deny, blame, justify and defend. They feel powerless, like their dreams have been lost or denied, and they're at the mercy of situation and circumstance.

Despite the obvious negatives, a victim can feel good in this position because they feel innocent. To the victim, everyone else becomes a persecutor – the bad boss, the disengaged employees, the unsupportive husband; even inanimate objects. Victims see illness and challenges – such as a cancer diagnosis or marriage separation – as persecutors; something they can blame.

Many people spend their whole life living from a victim perspective without even knowing it. Perhaps you identify yourself in this role. If not you, you're sure to know someone else who does. It might be your partner, a parent, a staff member, or even your boss. Operating from the victim position doesn't make someone a bad person, but it is a bad habit.

THE PERSECUTOR PERSPECTIVE

Often, people who start out as victims shift to another position on the drama triangle – that of persecutor themselves. As with the victim, a persecutor also focuses on problems, blames others and feels hard done by. But unlike the victim, they dominate, tear others down, and react aggressively under stress. Although this position is also damaging (to both the persecutor themselves and those around them), it can feel powerful, which is often why persecutors continue their destructive behaviour.

THE RESCUER PERSPECTIVE

And then you've got the rescuer. It may surprise you to find yourself fitting into the drama triangle in this role, just like many of my clients do. The rescuer is often the people pleaser. The person who tries to save the day, fix the problem, relieve the pain and make everything better. They believe they are doing the right thing, may feel righteous and can be a bit of a martyr. Often, they fear not being needed and while their intentions may be good, the rescuer unintentionally keeps the victim in the victim position, trying to save or fix them, rather than encouraging them to help themselves.

THE DRAMA TRIANGLE AND COMMUNICATION STYLES

Many people live their entire lives from one perspective. But some people move around all three positions, or shift in and out of the drama triangle entirely, multiple times a day!

Of the four communication styles we spoke about in Chapter 3 – aggressive, passive, passive-aggressive and assertive – all but one are characteristic of people who operate from the drama triangle. Can you guess which three? That's right, all but assertive communication can be found here.

People who operate from the drama triangle are not in control of their emotions and deflect personal responsibility. Most of the time, they have no conscious awareness of what they're doing – they're so used to blaming others they don't even think that there's another way. They don't realise they have a choice about their response.

But choice is what you do have – because there is another option; an antidote to drama in the form of an alternative model.

THE EMPOWERMENT DYNAMIC (TED)

American author and co-founder of the Bainbridge Leadership Centre, David Emerald Womeldorff, outlined this model in his book, *The Power of TED** (**The Empowerment Dynamic*), published in 2005 under the pen name David Emerald. In his model, developed as a direct alternative to Karpman's Drama Triangle, Womeldorff highlighted how a focus on choice and outcomes, rather than problems, could lead to a positive shift in the way a person approached life's challenges. If someone wanted to change their life, Womeldorff said, they had to create the life they wanted.

Figure 4: The Empowerment Dynamic

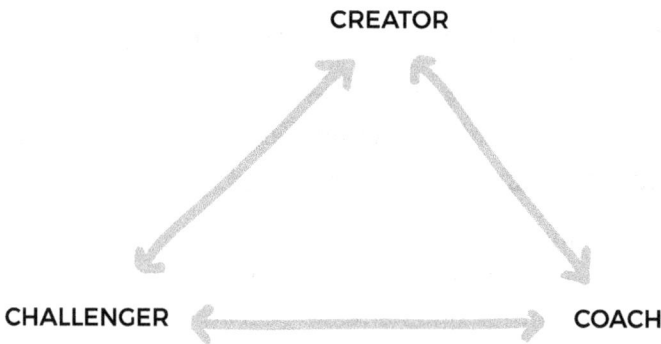

Source: Emerald, David (2005) *The Power of TED** (**The Empowerment Dynamic*)

THE CREATOR IS NOT A VICTIM

The Empowerment Dynamic (TED) features an upright triangle with three positions that mirror the drama triangle. But instead of victim, TED features the position of creator – a person who focusses on outcomes rather than problems and is conscious of their power to choose their response. By focussing on outcomes and end goals rather than problems, the creator is able to be resilient in times of challenge. They recognise that bad things happen to good people all the time and rather than let that consume them, they look for ways to deal with, remove or go around their problems. It's empowering stuff.

THE CHALLENGER IS NOT A PERSECUTOR

Instead of persecutor, TED has the role of challenger – someone who is focussed on learning and growth, who holds the creator to account while also encouraging action through constructive questions. Rather than pull other people down, the challenger builds others up.

THE COACH IS NOT A RESCUER

And instead of rescuer, it features the position of coach – a person who is compassionate; who supports, encourages and assists others but recognises they need to do the work themselves, because you can't help someone who won't help themselves. A coach will ask questions to help a person create their own vision and action plan.

THE LIFE-CHANGING IMPACT OF THE TRIANGLES

Assertive, measured, respectful and emotionally intelligent communication stems from a person operating in The Empowerment Dynamic. It is someone who operates above the line and owns their power to choose.

When I speak about the triangles in my workshops, I always see grimaces around the room as people identify which position they operate from. It can be eye opening and confronting. People often see themselves in one of the three drama positions, or at the very least clearly identify the positions of their colleagues, partners, family members and friends. I'm sure you're doing exactly the same right now – and if you're not, you should.

Stop for a moment and think about which triangle and position you most frequently operate from? Does your position change when you're under pressure? Be brutally honest with yourself, just like Andrew was, a dairy farmer from the Gippsland region of Victoria.

It was mid-2016 and the Australian dairy crisis had just hit. Milk processing company Murray Goulburn had slashed the price it paid farmers for milk, not only for future payments but retrospectively for the last 10 months too. All over the country, farmers suddenly found themselves working for a loss while managing massive debts. Heartbreaking footage of milk being poured down the drain rather than trucked for processing appeared on the news and tragic figures showing a spike in farmer suicides emerged.

Andrew had been a dairy farmer all his life. He came along to my workshop in Warragul on a Sunday afternoon, lost and looking for help to get him through this dark time. On top of the financial pressures due to the sudden milk price cut, Andrew's wife had left him. She told Andrew she'd grown tired of his unpredictable moods, negativity, and poor communication. She had also begged him to seek help for what she suspected was depression, but he had dismissed her pleas and interpreted the fact she thought he had a problem as her problem. His wife's departure had given Andrew the jolt he needed to seek out professional and personal development training for the first time in his life.

Andrew approached me during the afternoon tea break after I'd presented the drama triangle and empowerment dynamic concepts. He appeared energised and excited, so I was surprised when the first thing he said to me was, "I'm a victim".

"I'm a victim," Andrew repeated shaking his head, incredulous. "I've been a victim my entire life but I've never been able to see it before. My wife saw it and that's why she left, but up until now I've just blamed her and everyone else for the problems I face. I can't believe it. And I can't believe the power to change is in my control. I just need to make the choice."

For the rest of the workshop, Andrew's demeanour changed. He contributed to conversations and threw himself into activities. At the end, he described the session on his feedback form as "the most inspiring, eye opening, thrilling, heart racing afternoon I believe I have ever had". These models became the catalyst for Andrew committing to change his life.

The great news is, just as Andrew discovered, your position in the triangles is not fixed. Even if you've lived your whole life inside the drama triangle, you can make the shift into the empowerment dynamic. How do you move from one to the other? By making a conscious choice to do so and taking personal responsibility for your behaviour and communication. It really is as simple – and as incredibly difficult – as that. Never confuse simple with easy because this choice is one of the hardest you will make. Why do so many people live inside the drama triangle? Because blaming other people is far easier and more convenient than taking personal responsibility.

NO GREEN LIGHT FOR POOR BEHAVIOUR

"But why should I let them get away with it?" many people have asked me over the years. "If someone treats me badly, I shouldn't have to put up with it," they argue – and they're absolutely right.

Let me be clear: taking personal responsibility does not mean you excuse poor behaviour from other people. It doesn't make bullying okay. It doesn't mean you don't report harassment to your human resources (HR) department, ignore aggression from your staff, or put up with passive-aggressive manipulation from your partner. Not at all. You can and must address those issues.

Choice isn't about ignoring the wrongs done to you; it's about choosing how you respond. There's a significant difference. If someone is giving you a hard time, make a choice not to give them the satisfaction of feeling like they've defeated you. Make a choice to be the bigger person. Make a choice to call out their poor behaviour by reacting calmly, while standing up for yourself. Make a choice not to let them win.

"But that's not fair, Leah," some clients still argue. "Why should I have to be the bigger person if they treat me like that?"

My response is always the same: this isn't about other people, it's about you. Who are you as a person? What's your character? Who do you want to be? Make a choice and then have your communication style and response reflect the answers to those questions.

Do not let other people dictate your behaviour. **Do not give your power away.**

YOU ALWAYS HAVE A CHOICE; YOU JUST MAY NOT LIKE WHAT IT IS

Trudy was a nurse who worked in aged care. She spoke to me at the end of a training session in her workplace. She waited until the rest of her team had left the room before approaching me. Her story was one I've heard before.

"I know you said we've all got a choice, but I don't think I do," she said. "I've tried everything. I've tried standing up for myself, I've tried ignoring the behaviour, but there are two women in my team who have bullied me for the last six months.

"It's impacting my health, I hate coming to work and I've taken it to management twice now but they haven't done anything. I've even reported it to the manager above my manager, but still nothing has changed. So what choice do I have? What should I do now?" she asked.

I really felt for Trudy. What she described wasn't fair; it was awful. But she did still have a choice. If it was as bad as she said, if she had tried everything she could think of, if she had had the difficult conversations to no avail, and if she didn't want to report it through external channels, then she had to ask herself whether this was the place she really wanted to work. The choice she now had to make was whether to stay or go.

The suggestion surprised Trudy. At first she was defensive and argued that wasn't fair, that she loved working in aged care and shouldn't have to leave a job because of the poor behaviour of other people. I totally agreed with her. It wasn't fair. But based on what she had told me and what she was willing to do about the bullying going forward, that was the choice she had. It didn't mean she had to quit her job on the spot (not all people are in the privileged financial position to do that), but Trudy could reclaim her power by making a choice to take action by looking for a position at a different organisation with a culture more in line with her values. She could move onwards and upwards.

For the previous six months, Trudy had responded emotionally to the bullying. She'd let it tear her up inside, making her feel worthless, bitter and resentful. She was angry at the bullies, angry at herself for not standing up to them further and angry at management for not doing anything about it. This automatic, below the line response fed her perception that she was at the mercy of others with no power to choose and change the direction of her life. That simply wasn't true. She was not powerless. Even at this time of extreme hardship, she was powerful.

SO, HOW DO WE MAKE A CHOICE?

How you communicate and relate to other people is entirely up to you. It's 100 per cent your choice. But harnessing this power is much easier in theory than it is in practice.

To get there, you have to be prepared to take what I call 'extreme responsibility' for your behaviour. With that in mind, here are some practical strategies to help get there:

1. MAKE A COMMITMENT

Ask yourself, "Do I commit to taking personal responsibility for my communication?"

Think about it. Hard.

Do you commit, from this moment right now, to take responsibility for the way you relate to and engage with other people, regardless of how they behave towards you? If the answer is no, you may as well put this book down now and stop reading. I'm serious. Put the book down and go back to blaming other people for your communication and relationship problems.

The reality is that if you can't start from the premise that taking personal responsibility is essential to your success, you'll never be able to improve your communication in a way that leads to lasting and significant change. You'll always have an excuse. You'll always have a "yeah, but…" and as long as you give yourself that out, you'll revert to responding as you've always done, particularly under stress. That's why choice is the first step in the Five Cs model – because without it we can't go any further.

Taking personal responsibility for your communication and behaviour is not easy, but it's not complicated either – and it changes everything.

2. GET REFLECTIVE

Reflect on a time when you've had to communicate under pressure recently. Did you make a conscious decision about how you responded, or did you react emotionally in the moment with no thought at all? Could you have done better? What would you change next time? These are all questions to ask yourself if you truly want to take personal responsibility and choose to do things differently.

By reflecting on what you've done in the past, you'll get more conscious of your power to choose in the future. This brutally honest self-reflection is key. I encourage you to make it part of your every day. Spend a few minutes reflecting on your conversations, emails and body language throughout the day on your commute home from work in the evenings. As Stephen Covey said in *The 7 Habits of Highly Effective People*, "Until a person can say deeply and honestly, 'I am what I am today because of the choices I made yesterday,' that person cannot say, 'I choose otherwise'."

3. ADMIT YOUR MISTAKES BUT DON'T BEAT YOURSELF UP

Personal responsibility is not about punishing yourself for your poor communication choices. 'Owning' your responsibility does not mean you torture yourself with feelings of guilt and self-doubt forever afterwards. That will only keep you in a victim mindset. Owning your behaviour simply means reflecting on and acknowledging what you did – good or bad – and understanding that you have the power to choose a different response next time.

The reality is that you won't get your communication right all the time. You will stuff up. You're human after all. The key is to forget the mistake but remember the lesson – and then move on.

4. KNOW WHO YOU ARE AND WHO YOU WANT TO BE

To be able to make a choice about how you want to communicate, you first need to know who you really are and what you stand for. How do you communicate now? How do you want to communicate in the future? What are you striving for? How do you want to be known? How do you want to behave? What sort of character do you have? Who are you? It's difficult to make a choice about how to stand up, if you don't know what you stand for.

In *The Subtle Art of Not Giving a F*ck*, Mark Manson said: "Honest self-questioning is difficult. It requires asking yourself simple questions that are uncomfortable to answer." He's right and it's essential to your success.

5. BE CLEAR ON YOUR VALUES

What values are the most important to how you live your life? What is core to you as a human? Can you articulate your top three and what they actually mean? If you haven't done a personal values exercise before, now is the time to do one. I'm not asking you to come up with some airy-fairy feelgood concepts to stick on a wall and ignore. I'm asking you to think deeply about what you value most in your life. These core values are essential for you to be your authentic self.

Why is this important? Knowing your core values and living in alignment with them will give you clarity about how you communicate and make decision-making much easier.

Knowing your values also helps you identify your 'line in the sand' – the line you are not prepared to cross. You'll know when you're prepared to stay silent and when you are compelled to stand up, even when it's uncomfortable. Sometimes it's hard to speak up for what you believe in but when you're clear on your values, this becomes much easier.

When you know where that line is for you, it's not a question of 'do I' or 'don't I'? You just do. For example, I value equality and detest discrimination. If I see or hear something that breaks this value, I'll always call it out. I'll do so calmly and assertively but I always do it. It's not always easy. In fact, it's often awkward and uncomfortable, because my value may not match the person I'm speaking to. The response from others is often defensive, like the friend who said his use of the word 'retard' was okay because that's how people in the construction industry talk.

But you know what? The other person's response doesn't matter. It's not about them, it's about me, and for me to live in line with my values, it's what I need to do.

Living in alignment with your values also reduces stress. If you value honesty but won't listen to or give constructive feedback, something will feel off – even if you can't articulate it. When you know your values – and live by them – you won't feel this unease. You won't beat yourself up all the time. You won't feel stressed that your behaviour is out of line with what you say is important to you. Because it won't be. Instead, you'll feel comfortable that you're living authentically and be calmer as a result.

There are thousands of tools online to help you determine your values and I've got one too. Set aside some time and go to leahmether.com.au for your free download.

6. GET CONSCIOUS

It's easy to say you'll stop and choose how you communicate but it's another thing entirely to do it in the moment when you're under pressure. So how do you get better at making a choice to take the high road when someone's yelling at you or manipulating a situation? You get conscious, that's how.

Rather than communicate on autopilot, you get conscious of being in the moment and thinking about what you're doing before you do it. You get conscious of that magic quarter second. In other words, you get mindful.

Stay with me here because mindfulness is not an airy-fairy concept. Its benefits are proven for everything from reducing stress, improving productivity and focus, increasing resilience and strengthening relationships.

Mindfulness is about focussing on the present. It's paying full attention to what's going on in and outside you without judging. It means you observe your thoughts and feelings and are fully aware of your reaction. Although mindfulness stems from Buddhist meditation principles, I'm not suggesting you stop and meditate anytime you have to communicate with someone. That would be impractical. What I am suggesting is that you take a breath. Train yourself to take a deep, mindful, conscious breath before you open your mouth and use that action as your reminder to choose how you respond. You might even practice saying the word 'breathe' in your head as you do it, to really bring yourself into the moment and use that brief moment to choose a response.

Alternatively, you may like to use your sense of touch to spark your consciousness and remind you of your choice. It might be squeezing your little finger or the pressure point in the webbing of your thumb and first finger to ground you in the present. Whatever it is, pick a physical action to remind you of your choice.

7. LEARN TO FORGIVE.

This is a tough one, but you'll never be able to move from a victim mindset if you can't stop blaming other people and holding onto anger and frustration. We're all human. We all make mistakes. We are all emotional beings. And while you now have the benefit of understanding the power of choice, many people don't.

As I said earlier, many people go through their whole lives operating from a victim perspective and then wonder why things didn't work out for them. Rather than get angry when someone communicates poorly with you, or cuts you down, let go of vindictiveness and revenge and rise above it.

Holding onto these emotions might feel good in the short term but they don't serve you. They don't allow you the clarity you need to consciously choose your best response. Embrace Disney's *Frozen* and in the words of Elsa, "Let it go."

8. FOCUS ON OUTCOMES

When challenges and roadblocks arise – and they will – challenge yourself to think of the outcome you want, rather than focusing on the problem you have. The problem will still be there either way, but by focussing on the outcome you're more likely to find a way around it. This will help you maintain resilience through that challenging time and communicate effectively along the way.

For example, focussing on the poor financial position of your small business will likely have you circling the problem for weeks, stewing over budgets, holding meetings with a lot of talk but little action, a rapid drop in morale, and a resulting lack of trust in your leadership. Alternatively, if you acknowledge the problem but then quickly move to focus on the outcome you want, you're likely to shift your team's thinking into finding strategic solutions to steer you through the challenge and help turn the poor result around, all while instilling confidence in your leadership.

Chapter 6

CONTROL

While choice may be the crucial first step in the Five C model, it is followed closely by control – specifically, by your ability to have control of your response in any given situation. To put your choice into action, you must be able to control what you say and do.

Control is about being able to regulate your response and communicate your emotions in a deliberate and intentional way. It's about controlling your emotions, rather than letting them control you. It's letting someone know you're angry, frustrated or disappointed without screaming in their face. And if you do scream, it's because you consciously decide to.

You'll never be able to communicate effectively under pressure if you're a pinball to your emotions and circumstance. Maybe you bottle up your feelings and explode, cry the minute you're challenged, snap aggressively when stressed, or get defensive when someone gives you feedback. These responses will all have a negative impact on your communication, whether or not you achieve the outcome you want, and how others perceive you.

That doesn't mean you shouldn't show feeling or emotion – vulnerability plays a crucial role in fostering connection, trust and respect. But it does mean learning how to communicate consciously. It means being deliberate in your response and managing yourself so that you can communicate and express how you feel in the way you choose. Rather than communicating as a reaction, you are in control.

A lack of control is why many people struggle to implement specific communication skills, such as active listening, receiving difficult feedback, or delivering an unpopular message. Although they know what to do, they can't put it into practice. Knowing and doing are two very different things.

Your competency to do your job – particularly if you're a leader – will be judged against how you control your reactions and emotions. It may even be what holds you back from getting a job in the first place. I know people who have missed out on promotions, not because they lacked experience but because they lacked the ability to stay calm under pressure. It's one of the core competencies for a good leader. Again, it will often be your soft skills, and not your technical ability, that will be your undoing.

A person who lacks control of their communication will quickly lose the respect of their colleagues, undermine people's faith in their competency, and negatively impact the performance of those around them.

CONTROL YOUR 'CONTROLLABLES' AND LET THE REST GO

However, control in communication is about more than just being able to control your emotions. It's also about focussing on what is **within** your control and letting go of the rest. Too often we waste precious time and energy worrying about things we have no control over, and all this does is undermine our confidence and ability to do a job well.

Not only is it ineffective, it can also be damaging to your emotional health. You might stress about what your boss thinks of a report you submitted, overthink what colleagues could be saying behind your back, or worry about how a staff member will take the feedback you have to give them. And guess what? That does nothing to change the outcome of any of these situations because you have absolutely no control over them.

Below is a simple list of what is within your control when it comes to communication and what's not.

Within your control:

- Your response to other people, situations and circumstances – this is about your choice to communicate above or below the line (see page 57)
- How you display your emotions
- The way you communicate
- Your body language
- Your mood
- The energy you bring to communicating
- The preparation you do ahead of initiating communication
- Your commitment to and practice of skills to improve your communication.

Outside your control:

- How other people respond to you and your communication
- What other people think of you
- What other people say or do
- Many of the things that happen to you in life (situations and circumstance)
- Other people's emotions
- The meaning people give to what you say
- What people hear.

You can't control a lot of what happens in your life, you can only control your response to it. You can't control your company making everyone redundant, nor can you control a cancer diagnosis. What you can control is how you react to the news and what you do in the aftermath.

You can only control you. You can't control how people respond to your communication. No matter how fair and reasonable you are, someone may get offended by what you say or react poorly. You can only control how you deliver the message. You can be considerate (see Chapter 7) and calm but they might still yell and scream. If they do, that's about them, not you. Your aim is to communicate in the best way possible and then let the chips fall where they may.

You can't please everyone all the time. To the people pleasers reading this book, know this: you will fail. There's nothing more certain. You can't please all people all the time and you'll tie yourself in knots trying.

You also can't control what other people think of you. No matter how nice you are, some people won't like you. It's just a reality of life and the sooner you learn to accept it, the sooner you'll succeed. Some people may not like you because you're "too nice" and they think that's suspicious because it's not how they behave. We're all attracted to different personalities and not everyone will be your friend. That's okay. It doesn't matter if people don't like you. But it does matter if they don't respect you. Control in communication is key.

When I deliver a workshop, I'm conscious of the fact that I have no control of what attendees think of it. They may all hate it and if they do, that's something I have to live with and learn from (thankfully that has never happened!). If they did, I'd take their feedback on board and use it to help me do better next time, but I can't change their minds. I can't chase after them saying, "but what about that bit – that was good!" That would be weird. And stupid. No matter what I do, I can't control their response.

What I can control is me. I can control how I prepare for my workshops. I can control the content I create and the preparation I do in advance. I can control the energy I bring on the day, the way I present, and how I communicate my message – both through my words and my body language. I can control the time I go to bed the night before. That's pretty much it. I can control myself and I have to let go of the outcome.

I don't read too much into people's responses during my sessions. Of course, if everyone falls asleep then I have a problem. But if one person falls asleep, I don't take personal offence. I don't know what's going on in their life. I've had people attend my workshops straight from night shift. I've had new mums come along after being up all night with their babies. Them falling asleep may have absolutely nothing to do with me at all. I have to let go of their response and instead control my controllables to deliver an engaging workshop that keeps them awake – I must control *me*.

What do you need to let go of?

Consider your answer to this question after looking at the list of things on page 74 that are outside your control. Or make your own list. Split a page into two columns, one titled 'Can Control', one titled 'Can't Control'. Then think about all the things you worry about when it comes to communication and dealing with other people. Allocate each concern to a column. If it's within your control, think about what you can do to mitigate it. If it's outside your control, get tough with yourself.

Stop putting energy into worrying about things you have no control over. Not only is it a total waste of your time, but by investing energy in trying to control things that are outside your control, you are less likely to be able to control the things that *are* within your control. Your resilience will be depleted. Protect it and put your focus on things you can change.

CAN CONTROL	CAN'T CONTROL

WHY THE FLIP OUT IS A PROFESSIONAL FIZZER

I've seen many leaders in both paid and voluntary capacities come totally unstuck by their lack of control over the years. I've seen board members behave like tantrum-throwing toddlers and lose the respect of those around them over a basic difference of opinion. I've seen a meltdown by an executive over VIP seating arrangements, complete with foot stomping. I've seen someone storm out of a room and slam the door behind them because they didn't like the answer they got to a question. I've seen finger pointing, spit flying and someone get so angry I genuinely worried they were about to give themselves a heart attack.

When this happens, particularly if the trigger is something minor, my respect for those involved usually diminishes, as does my trust in their competency to do their job – all based on their lack of ability to control their anger and frustration. I'm not the only one who thinks this way.

Tracey, an industrial finance manager, lost respect for her department head after he yelled at her in front of other staff.

"He didn't like the advice I gave to a colleague, but rather than come around to my office and speak to me like the professional adults we're meant to be, he flew into my office while I had someone else in there, and just started screaming and jabbing his finger at me, telling me to never do that again," Tracey told me during a coaching session. "He totally lost it."

After he stormed out of Tracey's office, other staff went to check she was alright.

"It was so unprofessional, unnecessary and embarrassing," Tracey said. "I lost a lot of respect for him after that – particularly because I had another meeting with him that afternoon and he just pretended like nothing had happened. No apology. No acknowledgment of the incident at all. It really made me question his ability to do such a high-stakes job."

Like in Tracey's experience, respect for leaders is further undermined if there is a mismatch between the expectations they have for the way their team communicates and the way they communicate themselves. It's probably the most frequent feedback I get while running training in-house for organisations.

"My manager says they value honesty, but they're not open to hearing feedback and get defensive if I even ask a question."

"My leader wants us to behave with respect, but they blow up and yell whenever they're under the pump."

"My boss says communication is key to our success but shuts down and doesn't communicate with us when she's angry about something. She doesn't even say hello if we pass her in the corridor."

As a leader, your mood, behaviour and the way you communicate is contagious. It rubs off on those around you. If you yell and scream when stressed, don't be surprised if others in your team start responding to pressure in a similar way. If your anger is expressed in a dark and miserable mood, chances are that others in the office will become sad and miserable too.

Being able to manage your emotions and control your communication is crucial if you want to improve the culture of your team. If you expect your staff and colleagues to behave in a particular way, you must set the standard you want them to uphold. It starts with you. You must model the behaviour you want others to demonstrate – whether in the professional or personal sphere. You can't expect others to control their emotions and perform under pressure if you can't do that yourself.

If you want your staff to be open to feedback, you need to be open to feedback too. If you want your staff to communicate in a more friendly and positive way, you better be friendly and positive too. If you want to improve the behaviour of your team, you need to improve your own behaviour first.

Stop and ask yourself these two questions:

1. How do I want those around me to communicate?

2. Am I communicating that way myself?

Take a moment. Really think about it hard and honestly. Reflect on your behaviour over the last month. If there is a gap between your truthful answers and your desired answers, you need to work on controlling yourself and your communication first. You have to step up before you ask others to do the same. Make sure your own communication is in check before addressing the communication of your staff.

If you don't address your own communication first, not only will you lose the respect of those around you and negatively impact the culture of your team, you'll also negatively affect their performance too. At worst, your uncontrolled communication may make your staff incompetent.

Darren was the manager of a dairy farm and had a problem controlling his temper. He exploded in frustration when his staff made what he perceived to be mistakes, particularly if he'd already explained to them how he wanted the job done. He blamed them for not asking more questions and argued that the work was common sense so they should know what to do. The reason Darren's staff weren't asking questions was clear. It wasn't that his team was incompetent. Rather, they were worried about his aggressive and unregulated reaction if they did ask a question. Instead, they chose to stay silent. Because Darren couldn't control his emotions, his staff stopped communicating with him and, as a result, they made mistakes. He was frustrated with their 'incompetence' but didn't realise his behaviour was contributing to it.

When losing control is your normal, your communication also loses its effectiveness. People ignore what you say because your behaviour distracts and detracts from your message. When you lose your cool – regardless of how legitimate your message is – the focus shifts to your behaviour instead. It becomes about the yelling and anger, rather than what is being said. Instead of listening, people tell you to calm down (which usually has the opposite effect!), rendering the content of your message useless.

Take a football coach for example. A coach who screams at his players at every break loses his impact. Players stop paying attention and tune out. The voice just becomes noise. They don't listen to his words and this only adds to the coach's frustration.

WHY CONTROL IS CRUCIAL

People who are able to regulate their emotions and control their communications are more likely to make great leaders and colleagues. They are assertive, calm under pressure, decisive and stable. They manage difficult situations and resolve conflict effectively, they often put more thought into business decisions because they don't automatically react, and they lead by example.

These people are usually a dream to work with, and for, because their behaviour is consistent. You know what to expect from someone who can control their communications. You don't go to work each day, wondering which version of the person you'll get.

Some people argue that a person's ability to control their emotions and be resilient in the face of a crisis is ingrained. You either have it or you don't. While it's true that some people have higher emotional control than others, like communication it can be learned and developed with time and effort.

THE POWER OF STAYING IN CONTROL WHEN OTHERS LOSE IT

Being able to stay calm when communicating with someone who flips out is a powerful skill. Not only will it increase people's trust and respect for you and your ability to do your job, but staying in control often de-escalates conflict. If someone is yelling at you but you're able to stay cool and calm, they are more likely to come down to your level. It's hard to yell and scream at someone who doesn't respond in an aggressive way. You feel like a bit of a fool, hanging out there on your own, red-faced and out of breath.

Granted, this is not always the case – some people quite enjoy the power trip of yelling at others who don't yell back – but most people will feel embarrassed and awkward when they realise they are reacting poorly while you're maintaining control, particularly in a workplace environment. If you're able to control your response in the face of this kind of behaviour, you've got the upper hand, not them.

I have used this strategy many times over the years when dealing with difficult or angry people. The more uncontrolled someone's communication is with me, the more in control I get. I deliberately slow and deepen my breathing and channel my inner calm. I will not give away my power.

As a woman who has worked in a wide range of male-dominated industries, including power and water, this has been particularly important. While it shouldn't happen, physical intimidation by men towards women in the workplace is a real thing. I've found from experience that an ability to stand tall and strong in the face of someone else's outburst, then calmly call it out, has been crucial to my success at times during my career. When people know you can hold your own and won't engage in emotional and uncontrolled behaviour, they tend to behave better towards you.

My strength in this area was tested when I worked closely with landowners directly affected by a major project to build a world-first wastewater treatment and recycling system in eastern Victoria. Many were very unhappy about having the pipeline dug through their properties and argued the works would disrupt their farms and impact their businesses.

During our initial conversations, many started off with a vent – some yelled, some swore, the odd one even threatened. My response was to stay calm, considered and, most importantly, empathetic. This meant most landowners quickly regained control of their own communication and, after the initial outburst, would follow up with an apology, "Sorry, love (yes, most farmers still called me 'love' back then), I know you're just doing your job." Then our conversation would truly begin.

Occasionally, however, staying calm and firm has the opposite effect on an angry person. Rather than de-escalate the situation, it enrages them more. And you know what? That's okay. Maintaining control of your response is still a powerful tool, as it highlights their poor behaviour. If someone is yelling at a colleague in the workplace and the colleague is responding calmly, regardless of the issue and how right or justifiably angry the yeller is, they are the one that's likely to be in trouble. It doesn't matter what prompted the outburst, that behaviour is simply not acceptable.

By taking the high road, the person who stays calm is the one who will likely come out of the situation the best, with their reputation intact or even enhanced. They have demonstrated in practice their ability to perform well under pressure. The same cannot be said if they fire up and yell back. In this case, both people would likely be disciplined for poor behaviour, regardless of who's right or wrong.

CONTROL DOES NOT MEAN SUPPRESSING YOUR EMOTIONS

Don't get me wrong, being in control of your communications does not mean suppressing your emotions or hiding how you feel. It's not about turning into a robot who doesn't show any feelings. Presenting as a tin-man, like the Wizard of Oz character who didn't have a heart, is just as damaging as having no control over your emotions at all. This is especially true when communicating after a tragedy or emergency, such as a workplace death, accident, or fire that impacts the community; or with someone who has received bad news, such as a serious medical diagnosis or redundancy. You may be dismissed by your team as heartless, uncaring, cold and detached. People will find it difficult to read you and you'll create disconnect between you and your staff.

Suppressing emotions has a particularly detrimental impact when it comes to personal relationships. If you give your partner nothing in the way of emotional response, the relationship is likely to wither and fail.

Ignoring or burying your emotions isn't just a negative for the people around you. Controlling emotions to the point of not addressing them will eventually cripple even the most resilient person. It's important to allow yourself to feel strong emotions in order to move through them more quickly. Feelings of anger, sadness, grief, frustration and disappointment are normal. Denying them only delays and often increases their impact. Suppressing grief after the death of a loved one, for example, often prolongs the grieving process. While you may be stoic in the immediate aftermath, you fall apart years down the track because you haven't allowed yourself to work through your emotions.

Allowing yourself to feel emotions isn't a problem, it's how you express them that's important. As the Greek philosopher Aristotle wrote more than 2000 years ago in his classic work, *The Art of Rhetoric*, "Anybody can become angry – that is easy, but to be angry with the right person and to the right degree and at the right time and for the right purpose, and in the right way – that is not within everybody's power and is not easy."

EMOTIONAL INTELLIGENCE IS MORE IMPORTANT THAN IQ

The key to improving your control, and therefore your communication, is developing your emotional intelligence.

The term 'emotional intelligence' was popularised by researchers Peter Salovey and John Mayer in their journal article titled 'Emotional Intelligence', published in *Imagination, Cognition and Personality* on 1 March 1990. Salovey and Mayer's work was then catapulted into the spotlight by psychologist and journalist Daniel Goleman in his 1995 book, *Emotional Intelligence: Why it Can Matter More Than IQ*. In the years since, thousands of books, papers, articles, workshops, training courses and blog posts have been written on the topic. Research consistently shows that emotional intelligence is a strong predictor of success, good leadership and personal achievement.

Emotional intelligence (also known as EQ, short for emotional quotient) essentially refers to your interpersonal and communication skills. It's about understanding your own emotions and being able to express them effectively and appropriately while also understanding the emotions of others, and how to best deal with and work with them.

In the workplace, a high EQ is becoming as highly valued as a high IQ – for good reason. A person with a high intellectual intelligence is of little use if they can't control their anger and aggression, if they lack self-awareness and if they can't work well with others.

Emotionally intelligent people have high self-awareness and adjust their communication to work with the emotions of other people, creating a connection with those around them. They are balanced and measured and would never ask others to do what they wouldn't do themselves, and this builds their credibility.

Developing your emotional intelligence is one of the most impactful ways of improving your communication – particularly under pressure. If you invest in building your emotional intelligence – just as you do your technical competencies – your social skills, self-awareness and ability to control your emotions will improve exponentially.

THE FIVE DIMENSIONS OF EMOTIONAL INTELLIGENCE

There are many different models that attempt to capture the elements of emotional intelligence. The one I find useful is Goleman's from 1995, which outlines the five key dimensions of emotional intelligence: self-awareness, self-regulation, motivation, empathy, and social skills. He classes the first three (self-awareness, self-regulation and motivation) as personal competence, or how we manage ourselves; and the latter two (empathy and social skills) as our social competence, or how we handle relationships.

If you want to develop your ability to communicate effectively, you must focus on each of these dimensions. However, for the purposes of this chapter, our attention is on the first two dimensions: self-awareness and self-regulation.

Below is a representation of Goleman's model. I have paraphrased his descriptions.

Figure 5: The five domains of emotional intelligence

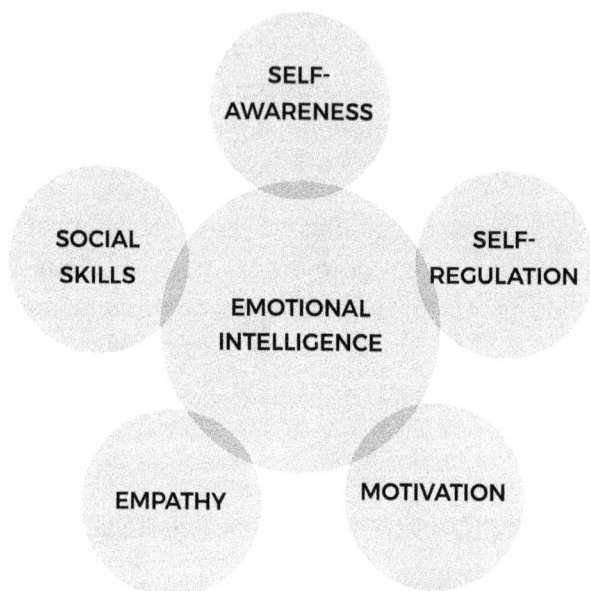

SELF-
AWARENESS

SOCIAL
SKILLS

SELF-
REGULATION

EMOTIONAL
INTELLIGENCE

EMPATHY

MOTIVATION

Source: Adapted from Goleman, Daniel, (1995) *Emotional Intelligence: Why it Can Matter More Than IQ*

Self-awareness: Your ability to be aware of your emotions and recognise how they impact your mood and behaviour, and the effect they have on others.

Self-regulation: Your ability to control your emotions and express them in an appropriate way at an appropriate time. People with high self-regulation are able to think before they act and adjust the way they communicate to reflect the emotions they choose to display.

Motivation: Refers to your ability to use your emotions to propel yourself forward. Your passion, drive and desire to pursue goals. Emotional motivation is what allows you to be persistent and resilient in the face of challenges. This internal drive will push you to continually improve your communication – not because you have to, but because you want to.

Empathy: Your ability to understand and be sensitive to the emotions of other people, to see things from their perspective and put yourself in their shoes – even if you don't agree with them.

Social skills: Your ability to pull it all together – to develop and manage relationships, built rapport with people, network, and seek common ground. These are your communication skills, usually in a social face-to-face setting.

As Goleman writes in *Emotional Intelligence: Why it Can Matter More Than IQ* (1995), "If your emotional abilities aren't in hand, if you don't have self-awareness, if you are not able to manage your distressing emotions, if you can't have empathy and have effective relationships, then no matter how smart you are, you are not going to get very far."

Don't forget to choose

But let me break in here, before I elaborate on self-awareness and self-regulation, and remind you that before you can even attempt this second 'C' of communication, you must first master 'choice'. You'll never be able to improve your control over your emotions and the way you communicate without first making a choice to do so. As Goleman said in his article 'What Makes a Leader', published in *Harvard Business Review* in June 1996: "It's important to emphasise that building one's emotional intelligence cannot – will not – happen without sincere desire and concerted effort."

So, ask yourself: do you have the desire? Are you prepared to put in the effort? If you do, buckle up, take a deep breath, and prepare for some honest self-reflection. What does that mean? It's a nice way of me telling you to not bullshit yourself. We get good at telling ourselves stories to justify our behaviour, but improving your emotional intelligence requires you to drop that mask and hold a mirror right up close to who you really are.

SELF-AWARENESS

At its core, the foundation of emotional intelligence and the building block to control is self-awareness. You can't change or control what you can't – or won't – acknowledge.

People who are self-aware know their strengths and weaknesses. They know their faults and their limitations. They know what triggers them to become defensive when challenged. They know that their enthusiasm and extroverted behaviour sometimes leads them to become a poor listener. They know if they hold a grudge, or they have a tendency towards vindictiveness if someone communicates poorly with them. They don't necessarily have control over these emotions yet, but they are aware of them.

People who are self-aware see themselves as other people see them. It doesn't come as a shock if others give them honest feedback that they find their communication style intimidating. While it probably wasn't their intention, they are aware of it.

The problem with self-awareness is that most people think they have a high level of it, even when they don't. Thinking you are self-aware does not make it true.

Sam was a case in point. He was sent along to my Effective Communication workshop by his manager because he lacked self-awareness and his communication style was impacting his relationships with colleagues. Sam was young and cocky. He worked in local government and had made his leadership aspirations clear. In fact, he'd outright told his boss he saw himself in her position in the next five years.

Sam was competent. He did the tasks required for his job well and never missed a deadline. But the way he presented himself, through both his body language and speech, was perceived as arrogant and was damaging his relationships across the organisation. However, he was totally unaware of it. In his mind, his behaviour was entirely appropriate. He saw himself as confident, professional, driven and assertive – a go-getter who knew where he was going and what he had to do to get there. If others were intimidated by his manner then that was their problem, not his. He couldn't help it if they were threatened by his success.

His manager was at her wits' end. She found him obnoxious and rude – and feedback from other colleagues was in a similar vein. Sam presented as a know-it-all; as if he was always right and others were always wrong. He knew best. Staff had complained about his patronising manner and inability to take constructive feedback. Senior executives had commented about him being disrespectful by regularly turning up late to meetings without apology, only to then check his phone multiple times throughout. His manager had tried to speak with him about it. She could see he had great potential to progress through the ranks, if he could get his communication and presentation under control. But while Sam had nodded and said all the right things in response, his behaviour had remained the same and it was rubbing many people up the wrong way. So here he was, in my workshop, doing a quiz on emotional intelligence that scored him on Goleman's five domains, including self-awareness.

Now, emotional intelligence questionnaires are not an exact science. Your answers will differ depending on how you're handling your emotions on any given day. The accuracy of the results is also determined by how honestly you answer the questions – whether you score yourself as you really are or how you wish you were. Despite this, there is often value in seeing where your results put you on the scale, even if just to prompt you to think about your areas of strength and weakness.

Sam finished the quiz quickly and while we waited for others in the group to add up their totals, I asked him how he'd scored. "Really well," he said with certainty and a charismatic smile. "My highest score was for self-awareness which I'm not surprised about at all. I really do nail that."

I considered this response. Interesting. Sam had been sent to the workshop because others believed he lacked self-awareness, but here he was saying it was his greatest strength. I wondered whose perception was right – after all, I'd heard two different sides to a story but hadn't seen the behaviour in action myself.

There was a chance Sam wasn't so oblivious after all. Maybe he did have good self-awareness and his manager had got it wrong. I was open to the possibility; stranger things had happened. I kept an eye on Sam for the rest of the workshop. He was engaged and enthusiastic. He said all the right things. I started to wonder if perhaps what was going on between him and his manager was more of a personality clash than anything else.

And then his phone rang. Now, I'm not the kind of presenter who tells everyone to turn their phones off at the start of a workshop. We're all adults and people are usually pretty good at managing their own behaviour. The reality is that sometimes we do need to take important calls or respond to messages during training sessions. But most people do this discreetly and apologetically, conscious of how their distraction may be perceived by others.

Not Sam. He stood and answered his phone. "Hello!" he boomed. "Yes, I'm just in a training session at the moment. Hang on, I'll walk out. Yeah, I'm well, thanks..." He didn't lower his voice, he didn't apologise, he didn't rush from the room. He simply answered his phone and started a conversation, while slowly making his way to the door, throwing it open, and letting it bang behind him on the way out.

There were 15 people in that workshop from a range of different workplaces. As the door closed behind Sam, every one of them had a similar reaction. Eyebrows raised, heads shaking, scoffs and looks of incredulity all round. "Are you kidding me? What a tosser," was the collective vibe.

Here was a guy who, not even two hours earlier, had been earnestly telling me how self-aware he was, behaving in a way that clearly demonstrated he lacked self-awareness. Sam had a real problem. He simply couldn't see the impact his behaviour had on others or the way his actions were perceived.

Worse than not being self-aware is thinking you are when you're not. Not all cases are as pronounced as Sam's though. Self-awareness is not necessarily something you simply have or do not. There are degrees of it. Some people will be very aware of parts of their behaviour that might be hindering their success but oblivious to others. You may be aware that you get angry when frustrated but have not delved into the reasons why.

That's something I had to do in my personal life.

Professionally, my communication is very controlled – I rarely let anything ruffle my feathers – but unfortunately the same can't always be said for me at home. With three young children, I found myself flying off the handle when the house was strewn with toys. I'd yell, infuriated they didn't pack up after themselves, and day after day the task fell to me.

I hated myself when I lost it. They were only kids being kids, but my frustration would bubble up after multiple 'reasonable' requests for them to tidy, until I couldn't contain it anymore and then BAM, I would explode. Do you recognise my position on the drama triangle here? I was very much in victim and persecutor mode. I still fall into them sometimes.

My blame was focussed on other people (my kids and husband). I wasn't taking responsibility for my response (they 'made' me do it; if they cleaned up I wouldn't have to yell) and my response was uncontrolled and, frankly, ridiculous.

Here I was, teaching people how to communicate in a calm and considered way, yet at home I wasn't following my own advice. I wasn't practicing what I was preaching. Something had to change.

I asked myself the hard question: What was REALLY going on? Why was I getting so frustrated and angry when my kids were just being kids? Why was my response so explosive? The more I reflected and forced myself to be brutally honest, the more I realised my uncontrolled response wasn't about the kids' behaviour at all. It was about me.

By nature, I'm a perfectionist. I like to be in control and have exceptionally high expectations of myself. While this has contributed to my success in many parts of my life, it has also been my undoing at times and was something I had to consciously work at to overcome.

What was really going on at home was me projecting my unrealistically high expectations onto three little boys and a husband, and then getting frustrated when they (kids then aged three, five and six) didn't live up to them. Understanding this was a lightbulb moment for me. It wasn't about them at all – it was about me. This new level of self-awareness also helped me regain control of my response (most of the time!).

Now, when I feel that rising anger and frustration with my children, I force myself to ask the question – is this really about them or is this about my unrealistic expectations? Of course, it's fair for me to want help around the home and to teach my children the value of contributing to chores, but the most effective way of achieving this is through balanced and controlled communication.

So how do you know where your own self-awareness sits? Well, you can take a survey or quiz online (although finding a reputable one is tricky) or have a formal behavioural or emotional intelligence diagnostic done, such as the Myers-Briggs Personality Type Indicator. But one of the most effective ways to understand if the way you view yourself is in line with the way other people see you is to ask them.

SEEK FEEDBACK

Seek feedback about the way you communicate and your strengths and weaknesses. Be selective about who you seek it from. Don't choose someone who will simply tell you what you want to hear or lie to your face. Choose people who you know will be considered, honest and courageous in the way they respond; people whose opinions you respect. Be brave (see Chapter 8) and ask a range of people – from same-level colleagues to your subordinates and superiors.

Present the request in a way that shows them you genuinely want to hear their feedback and be open to hearing what they have to say, even if you don't like it. You don't have to agree with them but it's important to at least consider whether their response does have some truth to it. That's what self-awareness is all about – being truly aware of how you behave, whether you like it or not.

Remember, your intention when you communicate with other people and their perception are two different things, and just because you didn't intend to communicate aggressively, it doesn't mean others didn't perceive it that way.

Asking people to highlight your weaknesses can be daunting but it can also be incredibly valuable.

Before you do it, though, here are some important things to consider:

- ▶ Only seek feedback if you're willing and strong enough to hear it. If you're going through a tough time or feeling vulnerable, now is probably not the time to actively seek personal criticism.

- ▶ Don't get angry or offended by the feedback. If you've asked for it and someone has given it, be grateful for the gift, even if it hurts.

- ▶ Use the feedback to help you improve, not to beat yourself up. The purpose of seeking constructive personal feedback is to increase your self-awareness and personal development, NOT so you can criticise yourself for not being perfect (remember, perfect doesn't exist).

When seeking feedback, you might script the conversation like this email I sent to 20 friends, family, colleagues and clients in mid-2018. Feel free to use it as a basis for your own:

Subject: I have a favour to ask and I'm hoping you can help

Good morning,

I have a favour to ask and I'm hoping you can assist.

I am currently working hard to improve my personal effectiveness and self-awareness to ensure I am the best version of myself for me, my loved ones and my clients. Although I am conscious of a number of areas I need to improve on, I'm reaching out to selected family, friends and colleagues whose honest opinions I trust and value.

I'd love it if you could please take a few minutes to respond to this email with two or three things I could do better. Essentially, I'm asking you to highlight what you perceive as my personal weaknesses.

If it makes you feel better and helps you to be more honest, you can tell me a couple of my strengths as well – but please don't feel you need to! I genuinely want your honest feedback, so please don't worry about hurting my feelings or offending me. Seeing myself as others see me and being aware of any blind spots I have is essential to my success.

Thank you in anticipation – both for responding to this email and for being part of my network.

> *Have a great day.*
> *Leah*

In the weeks after I sent this email, the responses rolled in. They were exactly what I'd hoped for: considered, generous and brutally honest. Some were difficult to read. Not because they were nasty or mean, but because they highlighted things that I knew I had to work on. The spotlight was on and there was nowhere to hide. Nothing came as a surprise though, which was a good sign for my level of self-awareness.

I welcomed every reply, knowing that for some people what I'd asked them to do had put them completely out of their comfort zone and been a personal challenge. It was uncomfortable for them too and also a risk, for although I'd said I wouldn't get offended, they didn't know that for sure. I am so grateful they trusted me to take their responses on board in the way they intended.

Once I had the feedback, the next question was what to do with it. How could I use it in a positive way that helped me strive to do better?

I started a Word document and re-wrote each identified weakness as an area for improvement. By the end, I had a powerful one-page document that I now read every morning as a reminder of where I need to focus to be the best version of myself. It includes great advice like:

▸ Accept help from other people.

▸ Don't overcommit.

▸ Let go and stop trying to do everything yourself.

▸ Slow down and breathe. Not everything has to be done at break-neck speed and it all doesn't need to happen today.

These words have power. Not just because I know they're true, but because they were compiled based on feedback from people I love, respect, value and admire; people who have my best interests at heart.

Not only am I more self-aware after sending that email, I started practicing more self-care too.

If you undertake this activity, make sure you give people time to really consider their response and then be curious about what they tell you. Whether you agree with them or not is unimportant. Understanding their perception of you is.

Once you have the feedback, your aim is to use it in a positive way to help you do better. I recommend doing what I did and rewording any highlighted weaknesses as an 'area for improvement' and compiling them into a summary document you can read over regularly to focus your brain and behaviour.

SELF-REGULATION IN PRACTICE

Once you have an awareness of how you communicate, an understanding of what is within your control, have acknowledged your weaknesses, can see how your emotions affect your behaviour, and have made a choice to do better, it's time to work on regulating yourself.

So how do we do it? If you struggle to control your responses, particularly under pressure, how can you put this newfound self-awareness into practice and ensure you consciously communicate? How do you control how you react and respond?

Here are some tips:

1. BE CLEAR ON YOUR MOTIVATION

You need to understand your why. Why do you want to be able to control your communication and manage your emotions better? Why is it important to you? What's the consequence if you don't improve in this area? Write it down. You must be clear on why you want to improve your control, as this will help motivate you to do the work involved. You need to clearly see that not taking action will be more damaging than doing the hard work.

When I asked myself these questions about the way I communicate with my kids, the answer to my 'why' was simple: to be a better mum. Controlling my communication is vital to ensure my children have a happy childhood where they know they're valued and loved. I also want to teach them how to regulate their own emotions under pressure and I can only do that if I lead by example. These answers to my 'why' are far more motivating than simply saying, 'I must yell less'.

2. KNOW WHAT PUSHES YOUR BUTTONS

If you know your triggers, you can build coping and calming structures around them. For example, if giving instructions more than once sends you into a rage because you feel like your staff haven't listened, a solution may be to take more time explaining the task in the first place and checking the person has heard and understood your request, before leaving them to it.

Or if you struggle to manage your emotions when you're tired, try to increase the amount of sleep you get. No one functions at their best when they're sleep deprived. You'll find this one action alone will have significant benefits on your emotional health.

3. DEPERSONALISE

Human beings often default to being selfish and egotistical, particularly under pressure. It's a protection mechanism that makes it easy for us to think everything is about us. Often, it's not. When Tracey's boss lost it and yelled at her in front of her colleagues, it was less about the fact he disagreed with the direction she'd given a staff member, and much more about how he was dealing with the stresses of his job.

Tracey knew this. She was confident there was nothing wrong with what she'd said, so she was able to depersonalise from his behaviour and retain control of her response. Yes, she was still angry and upset by his inappropriate and aggressive behaviour, but she had the emotional intelligence to understand it was about him, not her.

The reality is, we rarely know what is really going on in someone else's life. The colleague who snaps at you in a morning meeting may have had a fight with his wife as he left the house that day. The usually bubbly receptionist who didn't acknowledge you when you said hello may have had her dog put down the night before. You don't know the reasons behind another person's behaviour but it's important you understand it's not always about you. That doesn't mean you ignore poor or inappropriate behaviour, but it does mean you don't read into it more than you should.

4. EMPATHISE

Put yourself in the shoes of other people and try to see things from their perspective, even if you don't agree. Looking at an issue or situation from someone else's point of view will reduce the focus on your emotional response and help you further depersonalise.

This is what I encouraged the young members of a sporting club board to do after they were heavily criticised by an elder statesman of the club. The repeated criticism had resulted in multiple fiery confrontations, which had reflected poorly on everyone involved. Some of the board members had yelled in retaliation. Some had stormed off. Others had threatened to quit if the man's frequent criticisms didn't stop.

The board asked me for advice on how better to deal with the situation. The first thing I did was encourage them to stop thinking about their own offence for a moment and put themselves in the shoes of this older man. He was a long-term member of the club and had been heavily involved for years. He had recently retired after a long career as a successful businessman, where he'd held powerful roles on committees representing the community.

Now, it appeared he found himself adrift, struggling with his own sense of identity and purpose.

No, this didn't excuse his poor behaviour, but it did help explain it. With this brief exercise on empathy, the board could see where he might be coming from. Rather than retaliating automatically when the man next criticised them, they could see how focussing on empathy could help them retain control. They would still call out the poor behaviour but from a calmer position.

Next time you find yourself losing control of your communication, or reacting poorly to someone else, get out of your own head and consider what might be going on for them.

5. PUT A PAUSE BETWEEN YOUR REACTION AND YOUR RESPONSE

Take a break or ask for more time. When we start talking immediately, without thought or consideration, we are much more likely to react emotionally and without control. We start speaking before our head has caught up and, as the words tumble out of our mouths and our body language betrays our hurt, frustration, anger or disappointment, our head screams, 'This isn't even what I wanted to say!'

Too often we feel the need to react immediately to a situation or conversation and often when we do, it's not in the best way. Get into the habit of putting a pause between your reaction and response. Sometimes this may mean a physical break or asking for more time.

If a colleague bails you up in the corridor and hits you with a question you weren't expecting (figuratively, of course!), rather than um-ing, ah-ing or feeling trapped, try saying, "Actually, you've caught me a bit off guard. Can you leave it with me for half an hour to think about and I'll get back to you?"

Or perhaps, "I'm very happy to have this conversation, but I have a deadline to meet this afternoon. Can we schedule a meeting for tomorrow morning to discuss?" Or even, "I'm just on my way to the bathroom. I'll come and see you in your office in five minutes."

It's not about avoiding the conversation, it's about buying yourself some time to control your emotions and consider your response. Go and lock yourself in the toilet. Punch the air if you have to. Shake it off. Cry. Do whatever you need to do to let out your emotions and then think about you want to say. Take a few deep breaths and then go back to the person as agreed and have the conversation calmly, rationally and making sure you communicate your key messages clearly.

Sometimes it's not possible to put a physical break like this in a conversation. Perhaps you're in a performance review and just received unexpected negative feedback that you disagree with. In this case, walking away isn't an option but pausing before you respond is.

Take a deep breath and try a similar script to above. Something like: "Wow, that's disappointing and not what I was expecting. Let me process that for a moment." Or, "I'm just letting that sink in." Don't be scared for a moment of silence to follow. Breathe again. If you have a water bottle with you, add a further pause by taking a drink of water (I'm forever preaching the benefit of the 'water pause' to buy time).

Even just a few seconds to consider your response may mean you handle the situation better than if you launched into a reply with your heart and not your head. Better to take that moment to wrestle your emotions under control than to explode with, "That's crap!" and storm out of the room, only to have to apologise and grovel afterwards to make up for your outburst.

6. WRITE IT DOWN

Get your thoughts out of your head and onto paper. Rant and rave if you want to, but get it down, preferably on a notepad, or in a word processing file – not an email. This is not to be sent; at least not initially.

The act of putting your thoughts into writing helps blow off steam. Once you've written it (I find dot points are good), give yourself five minutes, then read back over it, crossing out the emotional reaction points and looking for the facts. Often, you'll find the first four or five points are purely your emotional response and point six is where you finally get to what the issue is actually about. Once you see it in black and white, you can determine where you're best placed to start the conversation and have a much better chance of saying what you wanted to say, not what your emotions automatically dictated in the first instance.

7. HAVE A CONVERSATION EARLY

Avoiding conflict doesn't make it go away, it only makes it grow bigger and when it does, it's harder to stay in control. When you seethe silently and bottle up your anger and frustration, you are more likely to communicate explosively. Your emotions build until BAM, you flip out. If something or someone upsets you, speak to them. Have a conversation early and nip the problem in the bud. It may be uncomfortable, but it may also help avoid a full-blown argument later on.

In addition to having the conversation early, initiate difficult conversations at a time outside of conflict. Don't raise complaints with your partner when you're already in the middle of a heated disagreement about another topic. Wait until you're calm and on top of your emotions to have the discussion.

8. ESCALATE WHEN NECESSARY

Rather than continuing to engage with someone whose behaviour or comments are out of line and risk losing control yourself, tell the person the action you plan to take, and then exit the conversation.

In a previous communications role, there was a particular customer who would phone and abuse me almost every week. He would bang on about the issue he had with our organisation; his manner angry, aggressive and threatening. Every week I hung up on him, but I did so without losing my cool and without fear of recrimination from my manager because I escalated the conversation and clearly told him what action I would take if he didn't stop yelling and swearing.

Him: "You're all just a pack of [insert expletive here]. You can go and get stuffed. I'm going to dump a truckload of sh*t in your driveway and see how you like it."

Me: "I can see you're upset Peter and I'm happy to have a conversation with you, but if you keep swearing like that, I'm going to have to hang up the phone."

Him: "Get f*&ked."

Me: "Okay, Peter, I'm going to hang up the phone now. Goodbye."

Click

Almost every week.

I didn't engage, I didn't get drawn into his anger and frustration. I put the ball in his court and made it about his ability to stay in control, not mine.

9. GET MINDFUL

As I said earlier, mindfulness is more than meditation, it's something that grounds you and makes you focus on the present. It helps reduce stress and anxiety and allows you to regulate your emotions and control impulses. It decreases the chance of you having a fight-or-flight response to people and situations, and instead allows you to be more logical.

Try introducing mindfulness into your everyday. It might be taking a walk, doing a workout, playing with a pet, deep and focused breathing, or traditional meditation. Not sure where to start? Download an app to help guide you through simple and quick mindfulness activities. Good ones include Buddhify, Smiling Mind, Calm, Headspace and The Resilience Project.

You can also introduce simple mindfulness practices at work. This might include avoiding email first thing in the morning to allow you to focus on the most important tasks without being distracted;

turning off all notifications on your phone, computer and laptop; and not multitasking. With these three changes, you will likely feel more in control, be more productive and be able to communicate from a position of calm.

10. PRACTICE

Being able to regulate your emotions and stay in control of your communication takes persistence, practice and time. My suggestion is to pick one strategy listed in this chapter and practice it for a few days before adding in another. Take it slow and steady. You won't always get control right and that's okay, so long as when you don't, you reflect, learn the lessons, and then try your best to do better next time. Remember, you're a work in progress – persevere!

Chapter 7

CONSIDERATION

There is no one-size-fits-all approach when it comes to communication. No right and wrong. No one way of doing things or rulebook to say: 'If you always communicate this way, using this style and saying these words, you will have success'.

It doesn't work like that. Why? Because no one thinks like you. No one. Even people you're aligned with and get along with well don't have the exact same thought process as you. Different people have different communication styles, preferences, backgrounds, life experiences, and truths that have shaped the person they are today. There's no such thing as common sense – it's not common to anyone but you.

That's why consideration is key. To communicate effectively with any person in any given situation, you must consider the best way to go about it and tailor your response to suit.

It's not about pandering to other people, being inauthentic or fake. It's about recognising that different strokes work for different folks, and your job is to consider what will work best in each individual case. Not only do you need to consider the person you're communicating with, but also the situation, culture of the company, position of the speaker, preferred communication styles, and how those styles work with each other.

While the focus of the 'choice' and 'control' chapters is on managing yourself, consideration is where you need to switch gears and focus outwards. It's not about you now, it's about them.

First and foremost, you must consider:

- The outcome you want to achieve through communication (rather than the problem you face).

- How to tailor your communication to give yourself the best chance of achieving that outcome (while understanding the ultimate result is usually out of your control).

BUT WHY?

But why should I change how I communicate, you may ask. I need to get my point across, and this is what I want to say. Why can't I just be direct and say it? Why do I have to worry about what the other person thinks? You've just spent a whole chapter telling me I can't control other people, I can only control me, but now you're telling me I have to consider them?

Too right I am. Even if you master choice and control, if you do not consider the outcome you want before having a conversation, or how best to communicate your message with that person, you will not be able to communicate effectively.

The hard sell, where you push your message and opinions onto others, rarely works. It just makes people defensive. Sure, you may have success with some people (people who are like you) some of the time. But you're just as likely to have disasters where your communication falls flat, doesn't hit the mark, or backfires terribly, doing significant damage to your relationships in the process. That's what happened to Karen, a team leader at a marketing agency.

Karen had to deliver feedback to two members of her team about their performance and ask them to put more effort into the reports they were preparing for management.

She didn't think it was a big deal and wasn't worried about the conversation.

"I'm the leader and giving feedback is part of my job. They weren't in trouble, I just needed them to lift their game, so that's what I told them," Karen said. "I'm an assertive person who likes feedback to be direct and concise, so that's how I delivered it to them – I just assumed that's how other people like their feedback too."

They didn't.

Karen's staff went above her and complained to her manager that she was too aggressive. The word bullying was thrown into the mix. That's how Karen found herself in my workshop; she'd been sent to work on her aggressive communication style.

At the end of the session, Karen shared her situation with me and was soon in tears. The bullying accusation had caught her completely off-guard. It had not been her intention to come across as aggressive; she had been aiming for assertive. She was mortified that her staff had responded that way and devastated the firm's management had backed them up. She couldn't understand where she had gone wrong.

The more I spoke with Karen, the more I could see what had happened. I didn't think she was guilty of being aggressive, and I certainly didn't think what she'd done was bullying. But that's because I'm an assertive communicator and I like direct, concise feedback too.

If she'd been telling me to lift my game, I would have responded to that style of communication well and appreciated her being upfront and not beating around the bush. What Karen was guilty of was not considering her audience and how best to deliver feedback to passive communicators before having the conversation.

She'd assumed her staff would take the same meaning from her message as what she'd intended. It's a mistake many people make, and it leads to conflict, confrontation, misunderstandings, disengagement and, ironically, miscommunication.

Intention and perception are two very different things. What you say is not necessarily what someone else hears and your intention may be very different to the way someone else perceives it – just like in Karen's case. While you can't control how they take your message, you can increase your chances of a positive outcome if consideration is a core step in your communication process.

Consideration can also help you further master control. By focusing on the outcome you want, you will often realise your first emotional response is not the best.

Tristan owned a function centre in a large regional town and had applied to his local council for a planning permit to increase the number of patrons allowed in the venue. A neighbouring restaurant objected, claiming the increased capacity would create parking problems and damage its business. Tristan was incensed. He declared war on his objectors.

The neighbouring restaurant fought back, posting about the alleged intimidation on social media. Further enraged, Tristan then posted passive-aggressive insults on his business pages in response. Staff from both businesses began slinging mud and it quickly began to damage their reputations in the community.

I spoke with the managers of both businesses separately and brought them back to the key question: what outcome do you want? When I asked this of the function centre, the manager answered quickly: "to get our planning permit approved." When I asked the restaurant, their response was similarly simple: "to have our parking preserved."

I encouraged them to focus on these outcomes and forget the personal attacks. When you play in the mud, you both get muddy.

Engaging in a war of words was only going to put the council offside and diminish their chances of being heard. It might feel good in the moment, but it would damage their businesses in the longer term. Their best chance of getting the outcomes they wanted was to play a straight bat and communicate their respective cases to the council in a considered, controlled and respectful way that demonstrated the validity of their arguments.

DO THE THINKING FIRST

Like so many things in life, success is in the preparation. The following pages provide you with an extensive list of things to consider before communicating – whether through conversation or in writing.

As you will see, thinking through each one can dramatically change your approach.

Things to consider:

1. THE OUTCOME YOU WANT, NOT THE PROBLEM YOU FACE

Focus on the outcome you want, not the problem you have or what your initial emotive response tells you to say. Look at the big picture. Understand your end game.

What do you want to achieve by having the conversation? What do you want to get out of it? The answers to these questions should guide the way you communicate. Want someone to understand things from your perspective? Yelling at them is probably not the way to achieve it.

2. WHETHER IT'S WORTH ENGAGING WITH THE PERSON IN THE FIRST PLACE

Pick your battles. Sometimes the best approach is to say nothing at all. It all depends on the outcome you want.

Whether you engage with someone or not is a key question to ask yourself when you're dealing with a manipulative person. These people may deliberately bait you in the hope you bite. They want a reaction – whatever form it comes in, whether reasonable or not. Sometimes, with these people, the best thing you can do is not engage at all. Ignore them and don't play their game.

3. THE ANSWER TO THE FOLLOWING THREE QUESTIONS

A . **Is it necessary?** Do I need to have this conversation? Do I want to? Is it necessary to raise this matter at all, or not? Just because you have an opinion on something doesn't necessarily mean you have to communicate it.

Some things are better left unsaid if they hurt another person and don't benefit you. Imagine that a friend had a baby and called it a name you despise. Is it necessary to tell them you hate the name? No, it is not.

B. **Is it true?** If your communication passes the necessity test, the next question to ask is whether what you're planning to say is true and based on fact? Is it grounded in reality or is it just a story you're telling yourself based on the surge of emotions you felt in the moment? Is it your perception or is it a broader reality? If it's simply your perception, that doesn't mean you don't have the conversation, but it does mean you present it as such – your perception, not fact.

C. **Is it kind?** This doesn't mean the feedback has to be nice. It can still be very direct and confronting. But are you delivering it in the kindest way possible – especially if it is bad news? The aim is to stay hard on the issue but soft on the person, recognising that even the most difficult people are still people after all.

Delivering difficult messages in a kind way can help you retain respect and relationships, even during the most challenging times.

4. YOUR AUDIENCE: WHO THEY ARE AND WHAT THEY WANT TO KNOW

Who are you communicating with? What's their demographic and background? What matters to them? What challenges do they face? What style of language do they connect with? What questions do they want answered? How are you likely to best engage them?

Your audience and the answers to these questions should be at the forefront of your mind as you prepare for any communication. You need to know your audience and understand their perspective. It's not just about communicating what you want to say, it's about communicating what your audience wants to know, in a way they want to hear.

Too often, we are so fixated on the message we want to communicate that we forget to consider the people it's intended for and then we wonder why our message doesn't connect.

That's what happened in the early stages of the Gippsland Water Factory project, a world-first wastewater treatment and recycling system built in eastern Victoria. The initial key messages developed by the project team didn't hit the mark when delivered to the community. They were accurate, but they focussed on elements of the project engineers found exciting – things like world-first technology; an Australian first in waste-water recycling; and re-use opportunities for local industry.

These messages were great if you were explaining the project to technical experts, but to the local community whose water rates were doubling over five years to pay for the infrastructure, all they did was aggravate.

The first thing I did when I started work on the project was help rewrite the key messages with a community focus – something I could do as a local member of the community myself. I also asked other locals what they wanted to know about the project, and very quickly developed a list of the key questions we needed to answer in our messaging.

Instead of focussing on technology, we focussed on community benefits, such as the project treating waste water from nine local towns, removing raw sewage from the last open-drain sewer in Australia, significantly reducing offensive odour and freeing up fresh water in local rivers and lakes.

With this change in messaging, a change in community sentiment towards the project happened too. People still didn't like the fact that their water rates were increasing to pay for the project but, crucially, they could understand why the project was needed and how it would benefit them. We looked at the way we communicated from our audience's point of view, rather than our own.

You also need to understand your audience's motivation, values and drivers. What sparks the fire in your belly and gets you excited may not connect at all for someone else.

That's what Naomi found when trying to inspire her planning team to improve its performance. Naomi was a high achiever. She was a young, passionate leader with a strong internal drive for excellence. She wanted to create a high performing team that shared her vision for success. But some members of her team didn't share the same vision.

Chris had no interest in being high performing or improving productivity. He was nearing retirement and didn't care about toeing the company line. He was often late to meetings because he was caught up speaking with contractors and was known among the wider workforce for being unreliable.

Naomi was at a loss about what to do. His behaviour didn't conform with her expectations and her natural tendency was to tell him to lift his game because being repeatedly late was not acceptable. Naomi told me of her frustration in our coaching session. "I just wish he'd get on board. At the moment he's bringing the reputation of the entire team down and nothing I say seems to change what he does."

Naomi's own motivation was never going to persuade Chris to change his behaviour. The only thing that would was considering things from his perspective. What was his motivation? What did he care about?

As Robert B Cialdini says in his article, 'Harnessing the Science of Persuasion' from the October 2001 issue of *Harvard Business Review,* "A better approach would be to identify something the employee genuinely values in the workplace... That gives the employee reasons for improvement that he can own. And because he owns them, they'll continue to guide his behaviour even when you're not watching."

When Naomi considered Chris's values and motivation, it was clear: "Relationships with his colleagues and spending time in the field. He hates the admin, governance and meeting side of the job, but loves speaking to people and being outside. He cares what people on the ground floor think of him."

Bingo. Now we had something to work with. Naomi needed to frame her push for improved performance with Chris around his motivation to connect with people, not on her internal drive for excellence. Instead of telling him he had to improve his time management because it was her expectation for a high-performing team, Naomi needed to focus on the way it made other people feel when he turned up late to meetings.

When she explained that although it wasn't his intention, people felt disrespected and that he didn't value their time because he was consistently late without explanation, Chris finally understood his behaviour was damaging his relationships. He set his watch forward 10 minutes and made a concerted effort to get to meetings on time. If he was delayed, he would phone or email ahead to let people know in advance. He finally understood it was about respect and relationships, not time.

5. YOUR KEY MESSAGES: WHAT'S IT REALLY ABOUT?

Albert Einstein, the German-born physicist and celebrated genius who developed the theory of relativity said, "The definition of genius is taking the complex and making it simple." Einstein, the man who also developed the 'world's most famous equation' for mass-energy equivalence ($E=mc^2$), understood the importance of being able to simplify his complex messages to ensure they were understood by the masses.

Simplicity over complexity is vital for effective communication. Anyone can make something complicated. The real skill is to make your message clear and concise so that others can understand what you're saying.

In more recent times, Einstein's sentiment was reinforced by Apple co-founder and CEO, the late Steve Jobs, who said: "Simple can be harder than complex. You have to work hard to get your thinking clean to make it simple. But it's worth it in the end because once you get there, you can move mountains."

Before you communicate, get clear on your key messages and keep them as simple and succinct as possible. It's not about being patronising or dumbing things down; it's about being clear and concise, so your message is heard.

Can you explain your key messages in just a few lines? This is something journalists are taught early in their studies. One of the first lessons in news writing is the importance of structuring your story and ideas with the most important information right at the start. Start with the who, what, when, where, why and how, and then, further into your article, add the supporting arguments and evidence to back up your initial premise.

This 'inverted pyramid' approach doesn't only work in the newsroom, it's effective in conversation too, particularly when communicating a difficult message or complex idea under pressure. It's not about being blunt, it's knowing your key message so you can communicate it effectively without getting lost in unnecessary detail or roundabout explanations. It's about being able to answer the question: what's this conversation or communication really about?

Figure 6: The inverted pyramid

Most important and newsworthy facts: what's the story/your message about?

The main story: what are the key details?

Supporting content: what background or supporting evidence/ information will help persuade and add weight to the argument?

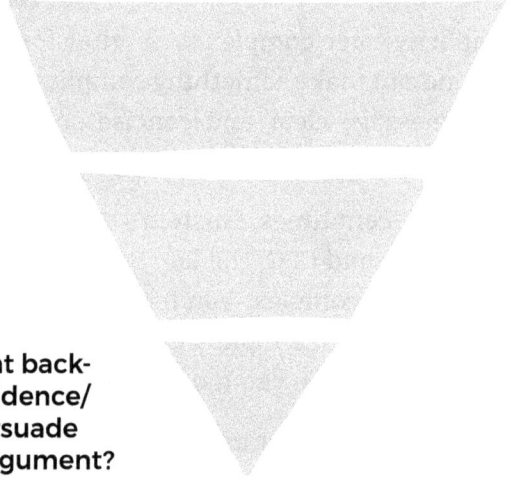

Source: Mether, Leah (2019) *Soft is the New Hard: How to Communicate Effectively Under Pressure*

Not sure what your key message is or how to sum up what you want to say? Then you're not ready to have the conversation yet. You have to do the thinking first.

So how do you know where to start, particularly if you are dealing with a complex issue with many parts to it? How do you know what the conversation is really about, or what point is the most important? That's where the barbecue test comes in.

6. THE TEST

The **barbecue test** is a technique I developed when working with engineers who went into excessive technical detail explaining projects to me that I then had to explain to the community. I'd ask them for an overview of what they were working on and they'd give me *War and Peace*: complex details that would leave my head spinning and without a clear understanding of what they were talking about.

After they finished, I would ask them to explain the project to me again, but this time pretending I was a mate standing next to them at a barbecue on a Sunday afternoon who casually asked, "Hey, what's that project about?"

The results were staggering. What they had spent 10 or 15 minutes explaining to me in detail, they often then summed up in a couple of lines. I now encourage all my clients to put their communications to the barbecue test.

If standing around a barbecue doesn't resonate, ask yourself how you'd explain your message to a 10-year-old child. Again, it's not about being patronising, it's about being clear and simple. As a journalism student, I was told Melbourne's *Herald Sun* newspaper was pitched at a year five primary school reading and comprehension level, while *The Age* broadsheet was aimed at year seven and above. This was to ensure the articles would be understood by the widest audience possible. It makes sense. By keeping your concepts and explanations simple, not only do you give your audience clarity, but as the communicator you have clarity too.

If it's a conversation you're initiating, summarise what you want to say into written dot points ahead of time and then scrutinise it. What is the best order to deliver the message in? Move points around, cut bits that are based on emotion rather than fact, and make sure you understand what it is you really want to say before you say it.

7. THE LANGUAGE YOU USE

Just as you need to keep your messaging simple and concise, make sure your language is clear and unambiguous. Don't use complicated language and explanations when simple ones will do.

One of the most common questions I ask my clients when they test their messaging on me is, "But what does that actually mean?" I usually have to ask it multiple times before the speaker is able to convey their message using simple language. Sometimes they are unable to explain the meaning behind their initial grandiose corporate statement at all, which proves embarrassing for everyone!

Plain-speaking is far more powerful than corporate jargon and waffle. It demonstrates confidence in your topic because you don't feel a need to hide behind big words to make you sound smarter. Remember, your aim is to have your message heard and understood.

That said, you should tailor your language to suit your audience. There are some environments where a more formal language selection is warranted and required, such as a courtroom. In other situations, casual and familiar is best.

8. THE BEST MODE OF ENGAGEMENT

What is the best way to get your message across? Is a verbal conversation the most appropriate approach or would an email or formal letter be better?

Written communication can serve an important purpose in high-pressure situations. The distance created by the written word can convey difficult or complex messages in a clear, unemotional way and give the reader time to consider their response. But beware: do not hide behind written communication to avoid a face-to-face conversation. While it may be an appropriate way to initiate discussion on a difficult topic, it will usually lead to in-person communications anyway, often with "Why didn't you just speak to me?" as the opening line. The other person may see the written communication as a sign of weakness and lose respect for you. "They're gutless; couldn't even say it to my face," might be the response.

Written communication also leaves it entirely to the words to do the talking. There's no body language, tone of voice, or chance to ask questions or clarify statements immediately. If not done with care and consideration, written communication can lead to miscommunication.

9. THE COMMUNICATION STYLE OF THE PERSON/PEOPLE YOU'RE SPEAKING WITH

In Chapter 4, I got you to think about what kind of communicator you are – in particular, what your go-to communication style is when under pressure at work. We looked at four main styles of communication – passive, aggressive, passive-aggressive and assertive – and how each style can help or hinder your success.

In addition to considering your own communication style before you have a conversation, it's important to think about the communication style of the person you're speaking with. Remember, no-one else thinks exactly like you, or communicates with the same style and preferences as you.

Considering your own go-to style and that of the person you're communicating with will significantly improve your chance of achieving the outcome you want. You can then adapt and adjust the way you deliver your message to best suit the situation.

Here's a quick summary of the basic dos and don'ts for communicating with people of each communication style:

Aggressive

As outlined in Chapter 4, aggressive communicators often disregard and disrespect the feelings and opinions of others. They are focussed on communicating their message however they see fit, without consideration for the person on the receiving end. They are often blunt, will interrupt and/or talk over the top, seek confrontation, and not be open to listening.

How to communicate with an aggressive person: Remain calm, depersonalise and empathise. An aggressive response often has little to do with you and everything to do with the other person not being in control of their emotions. Give them time out if necessary or, if the behaviour is unacceptable, you may need to call it out. Be assertive and stand up for yourself. Deliver your message in a confident, clear and concise manner that is to the point.

Don't: Be vague, unsure or over-explain – aggressive communicators are often impatient. It's also important not to get sucked into an aggressive response yourself (this will be particularly challenging if your go-to style is aggressive too, but make sure you persevere – assertive is much more effective). Remember, by remaining calm you will increase the chance they will drop down to your level and, if not, your retaining control will highlight their poor behaviour.

Passive

Passive communicators won't stand up for themselves, their rights or their beliefs, and sometimes won't speak up, even when they want to. They're often people pleasers who always say yes, apologise unnecessarily, talk themselves down and avoid conflict and confrontation.

How to communicate with a passive person: Tone it down, lower your voice and frame the conversation fully. Give them processing time and space to think about their response. Listen more and take the time to build the person up.

Passive people often have low self-esteem and battle self-doubt, so make them feel valued and tell them you want their opinion and why. Use their name and ask direct questions but be conscious of going gently or they will shut down. Reach out to them one-on-one in a relaxed environment, or through written communication where they can better consider their response.

Don't: Put them on the spot in a group environment or be too direct. If possible, don't rush them. Be conscious of coming across too strong, loud and enthusiastic. While you may consider your approach assertive, a passive communicator may perceive it as aggressive or intimidating.

Passive-aggressive

Of the four styles, I believe passive-aggressive communicators are the most difficult to deal with as they'll deny they're angry or upset – even if their actions and attitude clearly say otherwise. They'll also manipulate a situation to make you feel like the 'bad guy', give people the silent treatment, be critical behind people's backs, and play the victim.

Communicating with a passive-aggressive person: Let me take a moment to acknowledge how tough this one is, because the passive-aggressive communicator will deflect, deny and dismiss at every opportunity. However, if you want a chance at breaking through this wall, I encourage you to focus on what's within your control: you.

Create an environment where you genuinely welcome open and honest feedback without getting defensive, so that there is no need for someone to avoid having a difficult conversation with you. Consciously aim for assertive rather than aggressive and try not to let your frustrations boil over.

If someone's passive-aggressive behaviour needs to be addressed, make sure you address the behaviour rather than making it about the person. Say something like "Your behaviour suggests that you're angry with me. I'm very happy to have a conversation about whatever it is that's concerning you, but if you don't tell me what that is, then I won't know how to make it better and can't do anything to fix it." This shows the person the benefit of dropping the game and gives them an opportunity to open up and have a direct conversation about what's bothering them.

If, after this, the passive-aggressive person still chooses to behave in the same way, understand that this is their choice and go about your day. Focus on staying in control of your own emotions and choosing how you respond to their behaviour. Remember, you can't help someone who won't help themselves.

However, if the passive-aggressive person directly reports to you and denies there's a problem or refuses to engage in the conversation, it's now time to address their behaviour. You may follow up with: "Okay, if you say there's nothing wrong, I can only take your word for it. However, if that's the case, then I need to address your behaviour, because it is not appropriate." You gave them an opportunity to open up and they didn't take it, so now you have a performance issue to address.

Don't: Engage with it. Passive-aggressive communication often sucks other people into behaving the same way. It's lazy communication – juvenile and petty. No matter how tempting it is, don't lower yourself to that level. Rise above it by concentrating on your own choice and control.

It's also important not to play into the passive-aggressive communicator's hands by saying, "What's wrong? Why are you upset with me?" or something similar. Passive-aggressive communicators often want the attention – that's why many do it, to try and get you to work out what's wrong with them without them having to tell you. They may also be trying to manipulate your emotions so that you respond in a certain way (such as being overly nice and helpful to 'make up' for whatever it is you've apparently done wrong). This approach of applying your own meaning to the passive-aggressor's communication may also make them shut down or reply with something unhelpful like "you should know". Either way, your communication is not effective. Remember to make it about the behaviour, not the person.

Assertive

Assertive communicators are consistent and calm, appropriately honest and take a problem-solving approach to conflict. They don't shy away from difficult conversations, but they don't bulldoze the other person either. Rather, they walk the middle ground between passive and aggressive, having made a conscious choice about how they want to behave, and they are in control of how they communicate. Assertive communicators can robustly discuss and challenge different ideas in a way that isn't fraught with emotion.

Communicating with an assertive person: Be assertive back! Be direct, calm, reasoned and informed. Know your key messages and be respectful of the other person's opinion. Give them honest and constructive feedback – assertive people will take it on board and use it to help themselves improve.

Don't: Beat around the bush, talk in circles, internalise frustrations or be overly emotional. This will frustrate an assertive person, although in most cases they will be empathetic and controlled enough to handle it.

10. SOLUTIONS AND ALTERNATIVES

Before you have a conversation, particularly if addressing a problem or raising a concern, think about possible solutions and alternatives you could present in advance. You want to be the solution person and not the problem person, as this will increase your respect, influence and ability to persuade in the workplace.

Helping Jo take a problem-solving approach to her workplace challenge significantly improved the outcome of a conversation with her aggressive boss. Jo was feeling overwhelmed. She worked three days a week but had the workload of a full-time employee. She was worried she was falling behind. She had too much work and didn't know what to do about it. If she raised it with her boss, she was sure she'd be labelled as incompetent or lazy, so instead she was considering resigning.

"I can't go to her and tell her I have too much work on my plate," Jo said. "She'll eat me alive."

Jo was looking at the conversation all wrong. Instead of focussing on the problem (having too much work and not enough time), I encouraged Jo to look for solutions: a way of presenting the issue that would demonstrate to her boss that she had initiative.

I suggested Jo go home and make a list of all her work tasks. It was long and exhaustive but that was okay. Once she had made the list, I had her organise a meeting with her boss to discuss her work tasks and priorities. In the meeting, I coached Jo to approach the conversation like this:

"I wanted to meet with you today to discuss my work tasks and priorities. As you know, I only work three days a week, so I want to make sure I'm spending my time on things that require the immediate and important focus. Here is a list of my current work tasks (show boss the hard copy list) in the priority order I believe they should be in. Could you please tell me if this list is aligned with your view of what you'd like me working on, in order of priority? That way I will be able to best meet your needs."

Framing the conversation from a problem-solving perspective rather than simply raising a problem did two things: first, it highlighted to her boss the large number of tasks on Jo's plate. Her boss may not have been aware she had assigned so many jobs to a part-time employee and upon reviewing the list she may have chosen to delegate some of the tasks to someone else. Second, it increased the boss's respect for Jo as she had demonstrated her desire to try and best meet her boss's needs.

As it was, Jo's boss reviewed the list and agreed all the tasks did sit with the young woman but then highlighted the three or four main projects she wanted Jo to focus on for the next couple of weeks. She also told her which tasks could be put off until those urgent tasks were completed. It was a win-win. Jo felt less stressed because she had a clear path forward and, rather than feel overwhelmed, she now knew her priorities. And her boss was happy too. Rather than seeing Jo as a problem – someone who simply came to her with a complaint of having too much work and expecting her as the boss to solve it – she saw Jo as an employee with initiative.

Jo didn't cause a problem by dumping an issue on her boss to fix, she presented solutions to solve the issue herself.

Consider how you can be a problem solver. Look for solutions, suggest alternatives and think about what parts of an issue you're willing to compromise on before having a conversation.

11. HAVE FACTS AND EXAMPLES YOU CAN USE TO BACK-UP YOUR STATEMENTS

Focusing on facts and specific examples to highlight your key points will strengthen your communication, increase your chance of being heard, and make you more persuasive. Going into your boss's office and simply announcing, "I would like a pay rise", is likely to go down like a lead balloon. Without facts and examples, your statement is simply a wish.

But do some research beforehand and go in armed with facts and figures, such as what people within your organisation are being paid for similar work; industry standards; what people in other companies are being paid; what extra work you're doing above your current position description to warrant an increase; the achievements you've had in the role to deserve reward – and you're far more likely to at least get a longer hearing. Because you put the consideration into your message, your boss is more likely to give consideration to his/her response.

Go back and read consideration points one and 10 again and use them when negotiating pay – enter the conversation with a clear understanding of the outcome you want (as in, the specific desired increase) and also having considered alternatives and possible points of compromise. If your boss is unable to increase your pay, perhaps you could ask for an extra week of annual leave each year or a company car? Consider all of this before you enter the conversation.

12. THE 'WHY'

Putting the 'why' in your communications can be the difference between people listening to you and following your instructions, or not.

Whether it's in the workplace, your personal life, or dealing with children, explaining the why immediately increases the chance of people engaging with your message. It builds respect and trust, and often results in action – quickly.

It's a particularly good tool for leaders wanting to get team members on board with potentially unpopular decisions or initiatives, such as implementing a new policy or procedure.

If people know the reason behind a decision – although they may not like it or agree with it – they're more likely to understand and respect it. Simply giving an instruction with no explanation or context and saying "because I said so" just doesn't cut it.

In my workshops, I highlight the importance of including the why in your communication with a simple activity at the start of the session. I place three juggling balls on the table in front of each participant and ask them to stand up and juggle for two minutes. I give them no further explanation, no why, I just ask them to juggle.

The response is a great study in human behaviour. Some people take on the challenge enthusiastically, grabbing the balls and throwing them into the air with a laugh – whether they have any juggling skills or not. Others grimace and half-heartedly get involved, perhaps throwing one ball into the air to show they're following the instruction while looking unimpressed and clearly not giving their best. Occasionally, someone flat-out refuses to participate. They may stand up with the rest of the group, but the balls stay fixed in their hands. Some of these refusers avoid eye contact with me while others look at me defiantly, inviting me to challenge them. But I give them nothing. No encouragement and no explanation other than my initial instruction.

Often someone will question why they've been asked to juggle, or what it has to do with communication. To that, I respond with something innocuous such as, "I just need you to do it." At the end of two minutes, I ask everyone to sit down and I then launch into the start of the workshop, with no further explanation or reference to the juggling until four hours later.

In the second half of the workshop, when explaining to people the importance of including the why in their communications, I take them back to the juggling activity and ask people to tell me honestly what they thought. Common responses range from "I just thought it was a bit of fun" and "I thought it was one of those stupid icebreaker activities" to "I thought what the hell does this have to do with communication" or "What a load of crap." Because I hadn't given people the 'why' behind the activity, they had formed their own assumptions of what it was about and used these assumptions to decide whether to participate.

The same happens when you deliver any instruction or message without giving people a 'why'. While your supporters may respond enthusiastically and trust what you ask of them, others will jump straight to defiance, dismissing your instructions as unimportant, irrelevant or simply bureaucratic and without foundation.

The latter is what I did after my surgeon told me I had to give up running and jumping forever following double knee surgery for advanced arthritis in my mid-30s. At the time, I was a mad-keen exerciser with a love for obstacle racing and high-intensity interval training, so hearing my surgeon say I had to give up what I loved was devastating.

In my brain, the second he said, "Leah you have to give up running and jumping," I defaulted to defiance and internally replied, "Watch me". I leapt to assumptions. "He's saying that because he thinks it'll hurt too much. Well, I can suck up pain, I'll be fine," my defiant mental voice huffed. But then I caught myself. I'm a big 'why' person – I question things. And so instead, I held my defiance in check and said, "You're going to have to tell me why, or I'm still going to do it."

The surgeon nodded and then hit me with the truth: "You've got advanced osteoarthritis and it's bone on bone in there. If you keep doing high-impact exercise, you'll further damage your knee joints and be seeing me for total knee replacements before you're 40. The problem is that with current technology, replacements only last about 10 years and you can only get two in your lifetime. So, if you keep doing what you're doing, you're going to be in big trouble."

Oh. Righto. Suddenly, following the surgeon's instructions made a whole lot of sense. Instead of ignoring his advice, I was now going to listen. I was committed and on-board, all because he'd given me the 'why'.

The 'why' is also important to include when delivering difficult feedback. Why are you having the conversation? Be genuine and provide the 'why' to help the receiver better understand your intention. For example, if you're telling someone their performance isn't up to scratch, you may say something like: "The reason we're having this conversation is because I think you have great potential, which is why I need to speak with you about a couple of things that are holding you back." Approaching the conversation this way is more likely to result in the person being open to hearing the negative feedback, as they know your intention is to help them improve.

Don't wait for people to ask for the 'why'. Get in the habit of putting the why in your communications. If you want people to get on board, explain the reasons behind your decisions or actions – be they big or small, and whether you have to or not. And if you're on the receiving end of communication without a 'why', don't be afraid of asking the question yourself, but frame how you do so carefully so that it's not perceived as antagonistic or defiant. Try something like, "To help me understand the reasons behind the decision, could you please explain to me why we've taken that direction?"

13. THE LOGISTICS: TIMING, LOCATION AND ATTENDEES

Once you know what you want to say and how you want to say it, it's time to consider the logistics of your conversation (if it's one you're initiating, of course). What is the best timing for having it? Where is the best location? And who should be there?

The question of **timing** is an important one. There will rarely be a right time to have a difficult conversation, but some junctures are better and more appropriate than others. If it's a difficult conversation, often we find ourselves naturally drawn to having it first thing in the morning because we've been stewing on it all night and want to get it off our chest as quickly as possible.

But consider whether this is the best approach. While you may feel better having offloaded onto the other person, they must get through the entire day trying to hold it together, which can be incredibly difficult if they feel blindsided. If it's a Monday, they then have to get through the entire week!

Consider whether it would be better delivering the news at the end of the day and later in the week – perhaps Thursday rather than Friday – so the person can go home afterwards to react and process in their own space and time, then come back and ask any questions they have the next day. That said, if it's a conversation that needs to be addressed immediately, don't delay. Timing is something to consider but does not trump necessity.

Think about **how long you allocate** for the meeting or briefing. If it's a difficult conversation and you don't allow time to answer the questions the other person has, you may be accused of being aggressive, one-sided or uncaring. You're always better off allocating more time than you think is necessary for potentially tough conversations or staff briefings, and if you finish early, it's a bonus.

Location should also be a consideration. Don't have a difficult conversation in a glass office facing a busy corridor or open-plan office space, where people outside can glance in and see if someone is upset. Have the conversation somewhere private or perhaps even consider having it off-site, away from gossip and prying eyes.

Once you know your timing and location, the question of **who should be present** for the discussion is the final piece in the logistics puzzle. Sometimes one-on-one will be best – for instance, if you must give your boss feedback on an approach he suggested that didn't work. Other times, such as when someone is accused of bullying or behaving aggressively, one-on-one may not be appropriate and having a second person in the room to witness what transpires is important. Perhaps you should offer the other person the opportunity to bring along a support person or advocate too.

There is no one right or wrong approach in all circumstances, but it is definitely something you need to consider in order to avoid potentially big mistakes, like one that was almost made by one of my not-for-profit clients.

Tess came to me for advice after a volunteer was accused of being aggressive to her colleagues. Multiple people had complained about this person and the time had come to address it head-on. Thankfully, Tess ran her planned approach by me first.

"What we plan on doing is to bring her into the next board meeting and tell her that if her behaviour doesn't improve, we're going to have to ask her to leave the organisation," Tess said.

I stopped her right there. Hang on. This woman was accused of being aggressive and the plan was to put her in front of an eight-person board to tell her that's not okay? I don't think so. They'd be doing exactly what they were accusing her of – extreme aggression. You can't bring one person to face an eight-person firing squad and expect a good result.

In the end, I recommended Tess arrange a meeting with the volunteer attended by a total of four people – Tess and another member of the committee, and the accused and a support person of her choosing. It was important there were more than two people in the room to ensure the record of what was said was accurate and unbiased, but it was also important the meeting was balanced and didn't feel like a bombardment.

14. HOW YOU FRAME THE CONVERSATION

Consider how you can prepare the recipient of your communication for what is to come by 'inoculating' first. Inoculating is a term I first heard used in relation to communication by my colleague and friend, Maree McPherson, a leadership and executive coach, during a workshop we ran together for professional women. Maree adapted her use of the term from learning she completed with a company called Integrity and Values.

Inoculating helps prepare people for what you're about to say by giving them warning about what is to come. Think about the way police deliver difficult news. "I'm very sorry but I have some bad news…" or a version of that. This is inoculation at work. Before they even tell you what the news is, you know it's bad and can, in that moment, brace for the worst.

You might, for instance, say, "This is going to be a difficult conversation and there's a strong chance you won't like what you hear." This one-sentence introduction gives the person a chance to take a deep breath and steel themselves against what is to come. Even a few seconds to prepare gives them a better chance of controlling their emotions, as they know they're about to be hit with a difficult conversation rather than being smacked over the head with it and caught unawares.

Does inoculating lessen the pain of really bad news, such as a relationship breakup or death? No, of course it doesn't, but it can improve the person's response.

More importantly, does inoculating make the situation worse? For the deliverer, it might make the start of the conversation more confronting, but it gives the receiver a chance to prepare for what's to come.

15. THE CONSEQUENCES

Consider the consequences if the conversation doesn't go as planned. What will you do if the other person responds badly?

What would happen if you give the person feedback about their behaviour and it doesn't change? What will the consequence be if you tell them they need to improve the standard of their work and it doesn't happen? Give them this information. Tell them exactly what will happen if change does/doesn't take place. Be as clear as possible. For example, you might say, "If you miss another weekly team meeting without explanation, I'm going to have to give you a written warning. That means I expect you to let me know beforehand if you are unable to attend and why." By clearly articulating the consequences, you put the ball back in their court and force them to take responsibility for their actions (as long as you follow through!).

CONSIDERATION IS NOT PEOPLE-PLEASING

Before we end this chapter, please note: consideration does not mean always saying yes, giving in to someone else, or giving up your rights and opinions. It certainly doesn't mean giving your power away, changing who you are, or communicating in a way that doesn't fit for you. It is simply about giving yourself the best chance of getting the outcome you want.

While putting consideration into the way you communicate is essential, don't confuse it with people-pleasing. You're looking for the best way to present your message so that it will connect but, ultimately, how it is received by someone else is out of your control and on them, not you.

Chapter 8

COURAGE

You don't have to be a confident extrovert to communicate effectively but you do have to be brave. There are times when you have to be courageous enough to speak up, even when it's uncomfortable and even when you're scared or nervous.

As Maggie Kuhn, American social justice activist and founder of the Gray Panthers aged rights movement, said in 1977, "Leave safety behind. Put your body on the line. Stand before the people you fear and speak your mind – even if your voice shakes. When you least expect it, someone may actually listen to what you have to say. Well aimed slingshots can topple giants."

Maybe you hate conflict. Perhaps you're passive or shy and prefer to sit back and listen. You may have been telling yourself that you're not confident enough to have difficult conversations for years. It may have become part of your story, a limiting belief: 'I'm an introvert so I can't communicate well'.

Or perhaps you've tried and failed to stand up for yourself in the past. You've been burnt when communicating under pressure before, so now you avoid those conversations. Maybe you work for an aggressive and domineering boss and have decided silence is your safest option.

Well, I'm about to shake things up. You *can* communicate effectively under pressure, even if you're a passive communicator and even if you're scared. It's not about confidence, it's about courage, and it's time to get brave.

WHAT'S WRONG WITH CHOOSING SILENCE?

Silence has a place. As the famous quote (often attributed to British Prime Minister Winston Churchill) says, "Courage is what it takes to stand up and speak; courage is also what it takes to sit down and listen." Sometimes choosing not to engage in a conversation is the courageous option. Listening takes courage, and so does not being drawn into manipulative or aggressive conversations where the other person's aim is to spark a fight.

In my workshops, I encourage people to have the courage to own either their passive or assertive response. If something upsets you, decide whether it's something you need to speak up about or not. If you decide to speak up, do so in a direct, but calm and respectful way. If you decide not to speak up, to consciously be passive and silent, that's fine, as long as you then let the issue go. Don't hold onto it. Don't let it impact your behaviour or body language. Don't bring the issue up in two weeks' time. Acknowledge to yourself that you were upset but own your decision to not speak up. Let. It. Go.

But avoiding a difficult conversation or ignoring a problem in the hope that it will go away is not a strategy for success. Ignoring potential conflict doesn't make it go away, it only makes it grow until what could have been an uncomfortable but relatively simple conversation when had early, becomes a massive issue that ends badly for someone.

Leslie Perlow and Stephanie Williams explained it well in their article 'Is Silence Killing Your Company?' published in Harvard Business Review's book *HBR's 10 Must Reads on Communication* in 2013. Silence "doesn't smooth things over or make people more productive. It merely pushes differences beneath the surface and can set in motion powerfully destructive forces," they wrote.

When we choose to stay silent, we tend to shut down and distance ourselves emotionally from the person with whom we have the issue. We can easily fall into passive-aggressive communication and let our actions and behaviour speak on our behalf. As our connection with the other person weakens under the strain of silence, the cracks in our relationships can become unbridgeable rifts – ironic, given the reason many people don't speak up in the first place is for fear of damaging their relationships.

Sally was a case in point. A business manager for a small business in regional Victoria, she had put up with the demeaning 'jokes' of her boss for years without saying a word. He put her down in front of new staff, made sexist remarks, and was patronising about her intelligence in front of male employees. New starters took the boss's lead and quickly joined in the teasing, which Sally grimaced along with, while silently seething.

By the time Sally came to see me, she was a mess. Her choice to stay silent had impacted significantly on her confidence, job performance, and emotional and physical health. Thankfully, with support and coaching, Sally did eventually speak up – but more on that story shortly.

In addition to allowing conflict to escalate and creating emotional distance, staying silent can also have the following repercussions:

► **You'll be passed over for promotions and opportunities.** You might have the best ideas in the world but if you keep them locked in your head, they mean nothing. If you don't contribute to meetings or speak up with your thoughts and ideas, no one knows you have them. If you can't have the difficult conversation or address someone's poor performance directly, you're unlikely to be promoted to leadership.

Often people who take a passive approach to communication think their work will speak for itself. Of course it does, to an extent. If you're exceptional at your job, people will notice. But if you don't demonstrate that you can communicate effectively, you will be passed over for opportunities.

▶ **You become complicit to poor choices.** You're just like the 17-year-old kid who gets in the back of the stolen car with his mates. He didn't want to steal the car, but he didn't say anything to stop his mates either. When the police pull them over, the fact he didn't want to steal the car is irrelevant. He's in there and he's going down for the fall right along with them.

Versions of this scenario play out in workplaces everywhere. You're in a meeting and someone suggests an approach you foresee being a disaster, but you choose to say nothing. When that disaster eventuates, you don't get to say 'yeah, I was worried that would happen'. Your moment has passed. Instead, you are as responsible for the poor decision as everyone else in the room because you didn't say anything.

▶ **You generate feelings of stress, anger and resentment.** When you bottle up your feelings and don't communicate your frustrations; when you let fear of conflict hold you back from standing up for yourself; when you choose not to be courageous and instead let silence be your default, you do yourself a disservice, and you know it.

When you don't harness your courage and communicate, you get angry at yourself, the other person and the situation. And not just a little bit angry but that seething, boiling, resentful anger. Often it builds and builds and builds, until it explodes with aggressive communication that catches everyone by surprise. These explosions of pent up anger can devastate your career and personal relationships.

COURAGE EARNS RESPECT

Having the courage to communicate effectively earns you respect, particularly when delivering a difficult message or facing challenging circumstances. Nothing makes or breaks a person and their future career like the way they behave under pressure. While some people fall apart, withdraw, or go missing in action, others harness their courage and step up, communicating in a way that puts all five steps – choice, control, consideration, courage and communication – into action. As well as achieving better outcomes because of their actions and behaviour, those who are brave in such situations earn a level of respect that serves them well for many years to come.

Ron is someone who has demonstrated courage in a crisis multiple times in his 45 years at Yallourn brown coal mine in Victoria's Latrobe Valley. I've seen it firsthand – Ron is my father. As mining manager for nearly 20 years, he has led his team through natural disasters, union pickets and worker lockouts. He has experienced the devastation of a workplace death and was manager when a landslip caused the Latrobe River to flood into the mine for six days in 2006.

But it was the Morwell River Diversion failure in 2012 that best highlighted Ron's courage under extreme pressure and his ability to communicate effectively in a crisis. The man-made river diversion was built by engineering experts in the early 2000s to divert river flows around the valuable coal seam and enable access to new coal reserves. It was billed as an engineering feat and won an Australian engineering excellence award for its design and construction. But on 6 June 2012, the diversion failed, and the entire flow of both the

Morwell and Latrobe rivers flooded into the mine. It was a disaster. Thankfully, no one was injured or killed.

For weeks, a massive volume of water chugged into the mine, which supplies coal to the neighbouring Yallourn Power Station and generates nearly 25 percent of Victoria's power supply. The mine soon looked like a lake, with water first filling an area no longer in use before flooding into the operating side.

The company built pipelines, installed pumps and finally pumped all the water from the Morwell River past the failure and back into the Latrobe River. But it was 15 months before flows returned to that river.

For three months after the disaster, Ron worked 12- to 20-hour days without a single day off. He made decisions about what action to take, how to block rivers and where to temporarily divert their flows, where to pump the water that was in the mine, and what pipeline to build. He also managed communications with government, media and external agencies like Earth Resources Regulation personally.

Rather than hide behind a communications advisor, Ron took personal responsibility for communicating a difficult message in a timely, direct, open and honest way to the community in which he had lived his whole life.

Every day for weeks, Ron sent an email update to government and media at 6am. He followed this with face-to-face briefings with government agencies and journalists at 9am, and a second face-to-face briefing at 3pm. He provided all the facts and information he had, and answered any questions, being as transparent as possible and giving as much information as he could.

This made him vulnerable to criticism and personal attacks. He opened himself up as leader by showing his emotions in an appropriate way, fronting the media and taking the heat. However, rather than negatively impacting on his or the company's reputation, Ron's authentic and proactive approach saw him achieve the best public relations outcome available for the company in the circumstances. While the organisation took a hit with negative publicity (as expected with a disaster of this magnitude), Ron's transparency and empathy meant the community, media and government were well informed and understood the work being done to address the issue. They didn't need to speculate or search for a story – Ron gave them all the information he had willingly and he earned the respect of many as a result.

SILENCE GENERATES DISTRUST

The same could not be said for the company operating the neighbouring power generator, GDF Suez, during the 2014 Hazelwood mine fire, which burned for 45 days from 9 February and shrouded the township of Morwell with thick, choking smoke.

The fire was an environmental and health disaster, and the communications response from the leadership of GDF Suez could not have been more different. Rather than communicate openly with the community during the protracted emergency, the company stayed almost silent (apart from very limited and tightly controlled statements and information). Instead, it relied on government agencies and emergency services to do the talking – a 'one voice' strategy I am sure the company believed was right at the time, but that was poorly received in the community and was later investigated and criticised during the independent Hazelwood Mine Fire Inquiry.

The company was slammed for its approach in the subsequent inquiry report which described GDF Suez's communication response as "particularly deficient" (pg 384), "noticeably absent" (pg 397) and falling "well short of good communication standards" (pg 403) during the 45 days the fire burned.

The report noted that "GDF Suez did not issue a media release until 11 March 2014 – 28 days after the fire started" (pg 399) and criticised a "noticeable absence by GDF Suez at community meetings and media conferences" (pg 403).

Professor James Macnamara, an independent communications expert engaged by the Board of Inquiry to review communication during the mine fire, summed up GDF Suez's public communications strategy as "one that could be interpreted as showing disdain for the local community, and at best, showing a lack of sensitivity and concern" (pg 397).

While GDF Suez claimed its communications approach adhered to the state government's 'one source, one message' policy, this response was not deemed acceptable by the Board of Inquiry. It argued adhering to the policy "did not preclude GDF Suez from expressing compassion and empathy by having a physical presence at community engagement meetings and press conferences, or otherwise showing its compassion and concern for the community and the impact the fire had" (pg 403).

I felt strongly at the time, and still do now, that GDF Suez's decision to keep communication to a minimum and not have representatives speak at community meetings during the fire was a tactical error that damaged the company's reputation.

The decision to stay quiet did not look good. In my opinion, the company should have engaged with the community face-to-face, with a (preferably local) spokesperson attending community meetings, not to make an admission of guilt or liability, but simply to publicly express the company's concern and say, 'we hear you' and 'we understand this is a terrible situation and we're doing all we can to fix it'.

Trust and empathy are cornerstones of crisis communications. People need to feel validated, heard and understood. A time of pressure is not a time to be silent; it's a time to step up and be courageous.

HOW TO USE COURAGE TO IMPROVE YOUR COMMUNICATION:

1. TELL THAT LITTLE VOICE OF SELF-DOUBT TO SHUT THE HELL UP!

The biggest roadblock to our success is usually ourselves. It's our self-doubt, our feelings of inadequacy and that dreaded imposter syndrome. We all have that little voice in our head that says things like, "I'm not good enough. I'm not ready. It's not the right time. No one cares what I have to say. I probably won't get the job anyway. Other people are smarter than me. I don't deserve success. What if I fail? I'll probably just embarrass myself. People will hate me if I speak up. What if people realise that I'm a fraud and don't know exactly what I'm doing? What will other people think of me? Who am I to be that, try that, say that? Who am I?"

Some people hear that little voice of self-doubt and listen to it. The voice controls their actions and becomes their excuse for not doing or saying the things they want to. They don't apply for jobs or go for promotions. They stay in bad relationships. They don't speak up. They fear change. These people hear the voice of self-doubt and take it as a sign to stop.

But here's the thing: Everyone has that little voice. *Everyone.* It doesn't matter how confident, competent, or successful you are – or whether you're the CEO or a new apprentice – everyone has feelings of self-doubt, a lack of confidence and a sense of being an imposter at times. What sets people apart is that some are better at dealing with self-doubt than others.

To have the courage to speak up and communicate under pressure, particularly when your self-doubt is strong, you must first value yourself and your right to do so. This is a big one and, realistically, you're not going to address it simply by reading these words, particularly if you have spent much of your life thinking you are less-than. But know this: as a person, your rights are no more or less important than anyone else's.

When your self-doubt tells you otherwise and undermines your self-esteem and self-belief, you must stand up to that little voice. Talk back to it. Tell it to shut the hell up. Treat it like you would a naughty or sulking toddler – but with more swearing. Do this in your head or when no one else is around, to avoid looking like a crazy person.

The little voice is telling you you're scared? Bad luck, you're doing it anyway. It's time to be brave.

2. TAKE ACTION DESPITE NERVES AND FEAR

Just like self-doubt, nerves are normal. Don't be surprised when they turn up. Don't see them as a sign you should stop or avoid having a difficult conversation.

Nerves are a normal physical reaction to fear. When we get nervous, our body is flooded with adrenaline and cortisol, which are known as 'stress hormones'. It's a throwback to thousands of years ago. The fear response, wired into our nervous system, gives us the energy, speed and strength we needed to escape danger and threats – it's our primitive fight-or-flight response.

While this is useful when we are in physical danger, it's not so helpful when our fear is of something that doesn't have the potential to kill us – such as public speaking or delivering difficult feedback. Unfortunately, our body responds the same way whether the fear is real or imagined.

It's not a lack of confidence that stops most people from having difficult conversations, it's this feeling of fear. Therefore, it makes sense that courage and not confidence is what will help get you through.

The reality is that you will get nervous when you have to

communicate under pressure, it's a fact of life. The challenge for you is to manage the fear and have the conversation anyway. Avoid clinging to and overthinking your nervousness. Acknowledge it, see it, but don't hold onto it. Notice it and move on. Embrace the slogan used by global sportswear company Nike and 'Just Do It'.

Address the content of your fear and you will gain control over it.

Ask and answer these three powerful questions:

- What's the worst that can happen?
- What would be the reality if it did happen?
- What contingency plan can I put in place?

These were the questions I asked Sally, the business manager mentioned previously, who came to me for advice on how to deal with her boss's sexist jokes and patronising manner.

When I asked Sally what was the worst that could happen, she initially said, "I have the conversation and get fired." But when we explored this further, it turned out that wasn't the worst outcome. In fact, worse than speaking up and losing her job was continuing to stay silent and having the behaviour continue.

"I can't do it anymore. He's undermining and putting me down almost daily and it's having an impact on my health. The worst that could happen is for that to continue," Sally said.

Once she realised this, her decision was clear: She had to speak up. Not only that, Sally decided she had to resign. Facing her greatest fear head on by answering those three questions made it diminish in size. The fear of a particular outcome is often greater than its reality.

At the start of our conversation, Sally was nervous, apprehensive and self-doubting. By the end she was energetic and determined. She knew what she had to do, but she also knew that she wouldn't do it straight away and understood that didn't make her weak. It was a strategic move. She wasn't in a position to resign immediately, but she had a plan. That, in itself, helped change her outlook.

Yet while Sally seemed confident, I still didn't know whether she'd be able to follow through and have the difficult conversation with her boss. While I could support and encourage her, it was up to her to find the courage to speak up.

It was two months later, in December 2018, when I heard from Sally again. "I just wanted to say thank you for helping to give me the courage to have that difficult conversation," her message read.

"I did it and resigned. I feel very empowered and I'm proud of myself. I know the right job for me will be just around the corner and I will grab it with two hands and my new-found confidence."

Courage in the face of fear had given Sally the confidence she had wanted for so long.

3. HAVE CONVERSATIONS EARLY, BEFORE THEY BECOME CONFLICT

It seems counter-intuitive but if you hate conflict, one of the best ways to avoid it is by having conversations early, before the situation escalates. Addressing an issue quickly while it is small may make you feel uncomfortable, but discomfort requires far less bravery than confronting a major problem or crisis that has been left for months to fester and grow without being addressed.

Reframe your thinking and you will master early intervention. It is like ripping off a Band-Aid: when you do it quickly, the pain is over quickly; when you peel it off slowly, the pain lingers.

4. TAKE A NO TRIANGLES APPROACH

No Triangles is a concept developed by Rachael Robertson, the Australian woman who led the 58th Australian National Antarctic

Research Expedition to Davis Station in 2005, as discussed in Chapter 2.

At just 35 years of age, Robertson was in charge of 18 people, 24-hours-a-day, seven-days-a-week, for a full year (with the number swelling to more than 100 people in summer) in the most extreme weather conditions on Earth.

Robertson's strategy to keep the team strong and cohesive in such an isolated and challenging environment included the idea of 'no triangles'. It means that when you have an issue with someone, you have the courage to speak with them about it directly, rather than involving a third person and thus creating a triangle.

Robertson argues people create triangles actively – by speaking to a third person – or passively – by listening to the person with the issue. She says both erode trust and confidence and grow a culture of disrespect.

"The overriding principle of No Triangles is, 'You don't speak to me about them, and I won't speak about them with you – go direct to the source and have the courage to have a direct conversation',", Robertson writes in her 2013 book, *Leading on the Edge: Extraordinary Stories and Leadership Insights from The World's Most Extreme Workplace.*

I wholeheartedly agree.

5. BE HEARD (AND COVER YOUR ARSE)

Being assertive and having the courage to stand up for yourself won't always get you the outcome you want, but that is not always the most important thing. Sometimes you simply need to be heard. You may need your voice and message on the record because you need to cover your arse!

In the midst of the global financial crisis, around 2008, I was working on a public project that went over budget. The price of materials doubled overnight, there was union trouble and costs blew out. I was the communications manager. It was public money funding the project and there was a risk that news of the overrun would break in local media.

I was the youngest person in the executive meeting by a long shot, and one of only two women. One of the more senior and dominant men at the table argued the best approach was to say nothing about the budget blowout publicly and quietly work to bring cost overruns back in as much as possible.

I thought it was a terrible idea. As a former journalist, I knew if the story leaked (which it almost certainly would), the damage to the organisation would be enormous. We would be caught on the back foot, look evasive and dishonest, and have no control over the angle of stories pursued. We'd be at the mercy of the journalists, responding to their agenda. It would be a disaster.

So, I took a deep breath and said so. Although we would take a hit, I argued we had to put the news out proactively, openly and honestly. There were legitimate reasons for the budget overrun and we would have a chance to explain them if we controlled the messages. We could only do that if we released the story. Yes, it would still result in negative publicity, but we had a chance of minimising the damage this way.

Thankfully, after much discussion, the management team agreed with me. However, if they had not, my courage to speak up would have covered my butt. If I had said nothing out of fear and the story had blown up in the media, guess who would have taken the fall? Me – the communications manager. I was in the room for that meeting. I was a former journalist. Why hadn't I said anything? That's how the dialogue would have played out. My complicity in a poor decision would have led to my demise.

So, speak up. Even if people choose to ignore you or take a different approach, get your opinion on the record. Be heard and then document what you said in writing somewhere. In short, cover your arse.

6. DON'T TALK YOURSELF DOWN

In Australia, tall poppy syndrome is an ingrained and toxic part of our culture. By this, I mean that we cut people down if they are too successful, shine too brightly or appear 'too big for their boots'. Almost nothing is worse than others seeing you as a 'bit up yourself'. As a result, we're not only scared of failure in this country, we're also scared of success. We talk ourselves down before someone can cut us down. We are afraid of publicly claiming our achievements and accomplishments. We hold ourselves back and apologise, using words like 'just' or 'lucky' to diminish what we say and do. And it has an impact.

When you talk yourself down or apologise for your views, you put doubt in the minds of those listening. Unconsciously, people begin to doubt your ability and your competence too – even if you're good at your job. It's not fair but it's the truth. If you talk yourself down, others start believing you. You may miss out on opportunities and promotions or lose clients as a result.

Take the word 'just'. I used to use it to start nearly all my email communication. 'Just a quick email', 'Just checking if you've had a chance to read that report yet', 'Just wondering if you could get back to me by my 2pm deadline'. I didn't realise I was undercutting the power of my words. I was apologising for doing my job! When my colleague, Maree McPherson, highlighted my use of the word, I was horrified. I was diminishing my requests and instructions with this simple little word and, as a result, people weren't paying me and my requests the respect and urgent attention they needed.

If you're a busy manager and you get an email in your inbox that starts with 'Just a quick email', what do you do? You likely ignore it, leave it for later or, at best, skim over it. After all, it's 'just' an unimportant email. Never mind that I was on deadline for a critical media request. I used 'just' to soften my words in the misguided belief it was more polite and more respectful of others' time. In reality, I did myself a disservice.

Scrutinise your written and verbal communication. How often do you use 'just'? Can you remove it? Think about the way you introduce yourself. You're not 'just an accountant', you're an accountant. Be proud of your work; don't apologise for it.

Talking yourself down before someone else can cut you down is something many of us do automatically. An American manager pointed this out to me. He noticed the difference in the way Australians and Americans reported to him on the Gippsland Water Factory project.

"If I ask an American or Canadian person to write a report, they'll walk into my office with the finished product and say, 'Here is that report you asked for,' and put it on my desk," he told me.

"But if I ask an Australian to do it, they'll walk into my office and say something like this: 'Here's that report you asked for. I'm not sure if it's what you are after or if I've hit the mark, so please let me know if you need any changes or if it's not right. It's not my best work but take a read and see what you think.'"

By talking their work down, Australians put doubt in the manager's mind before he'd even read a word. Unconsciously, the manager picked up the report and looked for mistakes, rather than reading it and making up his own mind.

Be courageous. Even if you doubt yourself, don't put that doubt into other people's minds by talking yourself down. It's fine to seek feedback or offer to make changes, but keep it short and simple, like: "Here is that report you asked for. If you'd like any changes made, please let me know." Say it with confidence, smile, and then walk away with your shoulders back and head held high.

7. ASK FOR WHAT YOU WANT AND NEED

This sounds oh-so-simple, but few people do ask for what they want and need. If you need help from colleagues to meet a tight deadline, have the courage to ask them. Don't stay silent and wait for people to guess. Asking for help is not a sign of weakness – it's a sign of strength and good leadership. Sure, you might be able to do things yourself, but you'll only get so far and it'll often take twice as long. Ask for help and not only will you get further, you'll get there quicker. The strongest and most courageous people ask for help; the insecure do not.

8. STATE YOUR POINT CLEARLY.

People who lack courage in their communication tend to talk around topics and over-explain rather than have direct, succinct conversations. They speak in a vague roundabout way in the hope that the other person will eventually guess what they're trying to say. This indirect, laboured communication is often used by subordinates to their bosses, particularly if the boss is aggressive or the hierarchy of the organisation is strong. But rather than adding weight to what you're saying, being vague or over-explaining undermines people's confidence in your ability. You appear uncertain at best, incompetent at worst. The person on the receiving end also gets frustrated, often interrupting to urge you to "get to the point".

Vague communication is not only annoying, it can also be dangerous and lead to tragic consequences, as university professor and author Deborah Tanner explained in her article 'The Power of Talk: Who Gets Heard & Why', published in *Harvard Business Review*'s September-October issue from 1995. Tanner referred to a study published in *Language in Society* (Volume 17, 1988) by linguist Charlotte Linde, in which she examined the black box conversations between pilots and co-pilots before aeroplane crashes. One particular case took Tanner's interest: an Air Florida crash into the Potomac River that killed all but five of the 74 people on board.

"The pilot, it turned out, had little experience flying in icy weather," Tanner wrote. "The co-pilot had a bit more and it became heartbreakingly clear on analysis that he had tried to warn the pilot but had done so indirectly."

Tanner studied the transcript of the black-box conversation and found the co-pilot had repeatedly called attention to the bad weather and ice build-up but had done so in an indirect way to soften his communication because of the hierarchy of their positions.

"Look how the ice is just hanging on his, ah, back, back there, see that? See all those icicles on the back there and everything?" he told the pilot. And later: "Boy, this is a, this is a losing battle here on trying to de-ice those things; it [gives] you a false feeling of security, that's all that does."

Just before the plane took off, the co-pilot also expressed concern about abnormal instrument readings but, again, didn't press the matter: "That doesn't seem right, does it?... Ah, maybe it is," he said.

And then the plane crashed, and 69 people died.

It's not always easy to speak up and communicate in a direct and assertive way. Yes, sometimes you will be criticised for doing so by a superior or colleague. But if you think your plane is going down, better to stand up and speak courageously and take a hit for insubordination than to crash into the ground because you chose to be vague or stay silent.

9. ADMIT YOUR MISTAKES

Just as asking for help is a sign of strength, not weakness, so is admitting your mistakes when you get it wrong. Have the courage to put up your hand and say, 'I stuffed up'. Do so as quickly as possible after you realise your error. Apologise if necessary (sincerely), learn from it, and then move on. Don't beat yourself up. Don't dwell on a 'failure'. Dust yourself off and start again. Having the courage to admit when you're wrong increases the respect you're held in and creates an environment where others will feel more comfortable owning their mistakes. That is how you build a strong and positive culture – you lead by example.

10. SAY 'NO'

No – two letters, one syllable. A clear meaning. This word should be easy to say but for many, it's not. Learning how to say no is a challenge for the people-pleasers and high-achievers amongst us.

I struggle to say no myself. Not because I'm passive or intimidated but because I genuinely love helping other people and giving back to my community. 'Making a difference' is a core value of my business. Most of the time, that's a great and rewarding thing but sometimes I come unstuck because I take on more work than I should.

Being able to say no is a crucial skill. It is as important as learning how to say yes to opportunities, even when you're afraid or doubt yourself. It's a skill I've had to work on over the years and one that has taken a surprising amount of effort, practice and courage.

It's not just saying the word, it's *how* you say it that's important. You must be decisive. When you say no with uncertainty or timidness, or couch it in vague phrases like: "I don't really think I could", "I'm pretty busy at the moment" or "Could someone else help you?" you're effectively saying yes – and other people know it.

When I first started my business, I wrote job applications for people as a side hustle. As my business grew, I stopped doing this work. Except, for a long time, I didn't stop writing job applications because I was terrible at saying no.

Them: "Leah, could you please help me with my resume? I'm applying for my dream job and I really need your help."

Me: "I'd love to help, but I'm pretty busy at the moment."

Them: "Oh, but it's my dream job and it'd mean so much to me if you could help. Even if you could just read over it, that would be amazing."

Me: "When's it due?"

Bam. The minute I wavered, they knew they had me. Of course, I'd end up doing the work, feeling angry and frustrated at myself for saying yes, and often resentful of them for pushing until I did.

Kids work out this weakness even faster than adults. Why do you think they nag? Because they know if they ask over and over again, eventually mum or dad will go from saying 'no' to an exasperated, 'Oh for goodness sake, yes! Just go and do it'. Then, because they know it works, they'll do it next time, and the time after that. Adults are exactly the same. They know who will be a pushover if they apply the right amount of guilt and pressure.

"That's all well and good," I hear you say, "but how can I develop my ability to say no if I've always been a yes person?" Here are five techniques to help:

The broken-record technique

The broken-record technique involves restating a short, sharp message using the same words, much like a broken record that gets stuck repeating the same line over and over. It's a technique that requires some initial courage but, when put into practice, is very effective. It has certainly helped me.

If someone asks me to help them with a job application, my answer is clear:

"Sorry, but I don't offer that service anymore."

When they push ("But pleaaaaassseeee, Leah, I really need you), I repeat my position: "I'd love to help but I don't offer that service anymore."

And when they push again: "Sorry, I don't offer that service anymore and I'm at capacity with corporate clients."

They quickly realise they are not getting anywhere. I'm not shifting from my message and my position is clear. They give up asking much earlier than if I waver – and without the guilt trip!

Offer a solution or alternative

This option is perfect for those of you, like me, who genuinely do want to help others but still need to say no. Offer a solution or alternative to the person's problem that doesn't involve you doing the work. Give them a recommendation or suggest where they might find help elsewhere.

I often include a solution or alternative when saying no by using the broken-record technique:

"Unfortunately, I can't help as I no longer offer that service, but I can recommend someone else who does this work…"

When you say yes, understand you're already saying no

Time is a finite resource. Every time you say yes to something that takes up your time, you are already saying no to someone else. Increase your awareness of this. Before you say yes, ask yourself, 'By saying yes to this, who or what am I saying no to?' In economics, this is known as weighing up the opportunity cost.

By saying yes to a little favour for a colleague (which they should do themselves), you may be saying no to yourself and your ability to get your own work done. This could have a detrimental impact on your performance – your own work suffers because you're too busy doing the work for others. You miss deadlines and the quality of your work drops.

In your personal life, saying yes to an event you didn't really want to go to may mean you're saying no to spending time with your family. You run around pleasing people who mean little to you, while the people who mean the most suffer your absence.

Put the question front and centre: If I say yes to this, what or who am I saying no to? It's a game-changer.

Buy yourself some time with the words 'Let me get back to you' or 'I need to check my availability.'

If you are particularly prone to saying yes when under pressure, buy yourself some time. Pause between your reaction and your response. It's a similar technique to the one I discussed in Chapter 6, about pausing to control your emotions.

Try saying something like, "Let me check my calendar and get back to you." Go away and think about whether you truly want to say yes to the request. With the space to think it through, you can make a considered decision.

Create a 'no' checklist

For those of you who are such engrained people-pleasers that you'll still struggle to say no and need a fifth point, I recommend creating a decision-making process map or checklist. I created one for myself when my business took off and I went from chasing work to being overwhelmed with opportunity (a nice problem to have, but a problem all the same).

Rather than relying on the emotional part of my brain to make decisions, or pressuring myself to weigh up options on the spot, my business manager and I created a simple process to underpin the work we say yes and no to.

My process for saying yes or no to work:

- Can I do the work? (Do I have the skills or expertise?)
- Do I want to do the work? (Does it excite or engage me? Do I actually *want* to do it?)
- Do I have capacity to do the work? (Do I have the time?)

- Does it pay well and, if not, have the possibility to create future opportunities?
- Does it align with my company values? (Making a difference, zest, integrity, flexibility, excellence)
- Does it align with my business plan and strategy?
- Will there be consequences if I do or don't do the work?

I now run all work requests through this process to guide whether I say yes or no. It is not about me making the decision, my process makes it for me!

11. DON'T SHOOT THE MESSENGER

Few people enjoy receiving negative or 'constructive' feedback. Even when you know the other person is right, it is tough to hear. But receiving feedback is a vital skill for personal and professional success. It allows you to improve and develop.

What do you do when someone gives you feedback you don't like, or when they criticise or disagree with your behaviour, actions, or words? Do your hackles rise? Does your back straighten? Is your immediate response defence to their offence? Do you shoot the messenger?

To hear and consider difficult feedback takes courage. These tips will help you do it well:

Listen to understand, not to respond

Very few of us truly listen when another person is talking. Instead, we half-listen to what the person is saying and use the rest of our brain to focus on formulating our response. Our internal dialogue goes something like this: "When they shut up, this is what I'm going to say..." The result? We don't really hear what the person is trying to tell us because we're too busy focussing on our comeback.

Listening – really listening – takes courage. The courage to put our emotional and automatic response on hold and hear what is being said, even if we don't like it. The courage to be open to new ideas and perspectives. The courage and humility to recognise that our opinions, thoughts, and beliefs are not the only ones that matter.

In his White Paper, *Deep Listening – Impact beyond words*, listening expert Oscar Trimboli suggests there are five levels of listening that can help you move beyond just hearing the words:

- Listening to yourself
- Listening to the content
- Listening to the context
- Listening to the unsaid
- Listening to the meaning

How many levels do you listen for?

If you want to improve your listening, Trimboli has a simple and effective tip: breathe deeper. The deeper you breathe, the deeper you listen. So, next time someone is speaking, and you feel your internal dialogue talking over the top or your mind tuning out, focus on your breath. Breathe in for the count of four, hold for four, breathe out for four. Hear what they're saying and where they're coming from, then decide whether the feedback is valid.

You don't have to agree with the other person but always try to understand their perspective first and factor this into your response.

Drop the defence

Most people give feedback with good intentions, so drop the immediate defensive response. Instead of viewing feedback as a personal attack, see it as an opportunity to learn, develop, and improve. This can be tough. Many of us go straight to denial, blame or justification (the DBJs) when pushed outside our comfort zone or confronted with feedback we don't like.

Fight against that response. If the other person is being aggressive or negative in the way they deliver the feedback, have the courage to let their barbs bounce off you. Don't take their behaviour personally.

Be curious

Ask questions and be curious about how a person came to their point of view. If someone thinks you're a jerk, ask them why. Feedback is information – gather as much of it as you can. Probe. What is it about your behaviour that made them come to that conclusion? Why do they think like that?

The more information you have, the better you'll be able to respond and work out if their feedback is grounded in reality, or if they have made assumptions about you.

Ask for specific examples

Just as it's important to provide specific examples when delivering difficult feedback, it's also important to ask for them when you receive feedback. If someone thinks you're a jerk because you're 'always rude to other people', ask them to give you a specific example of a time you've been rude that demonstrates what they are talking about.

This will help avoid confusion and ensure a shared understanding of what they're referring to – even if you disagree. It will also give you the context to assess whether the feedback is valid or not.

Be grateful

Even if you disagree with the feedback you've received, be grateful the person gave it to you. No, you don't have to be grateful for what they said, but rather the fact they had the courage and decency to say it to your face rather than behind your back.

Knowing how someone perceives you or your actions is valuable information to have. Feedback is a gift. It opens your eyes to blind spots and gives you an opportunity to learn and improve.

12. REFRAME FAILURE

An intense fear of failure stifles many people's communication. Your fear of saying the wrong thing and offending someone keeps you silent, or your concern about embarrassing yourself in front of the boss means you don't put forward a suggestion about a new initiative.

So many of us see failure as a bad thing, something to hide from and avoid at all costs. That fear holds us back. Although failing isn't fun and often feels awful at the time, it's not the horrible monster we make it out to be. In fact, it's an essential ingredient to our success. Failure is how we learn. It's how we improve, grow and develop.

The most successful people in life often fail many times before they succeed. They take calculated risks, try, fail, learn, try again, improve – and repeat that cycle over and over. They fail their way to success. They persist and never give up. They fail over and over, and that is in fact why they succeed.

It takes courage to reframe your view on failure, but it's crucial if you want to communicate under pressure. You will get it wrong sometimes. Your words will upset people. You might not be as articulate as you wanted to be. But you did it. You were brave and had the conversation. That's not failure, that's success. No one is a perfect communicator. Everyone makes mistakes. It's only failure if you don't try in the first place, or don't learn from your mistakes. It's the courage to continue, not the experience of failure, that counts.

13. ESCALATE THE SITUATION AND MAKE THE CONSEQUENCES CLEAR

Having the courage to have a difficult conversation is a great first step, but if you find yourself having the same conversation repeatedly without achieving the outcome you want, be prepared to escalate the situation (see Chapter 6) and make the consequences clear (see Chapter 7).

The key here, though, is in the follow through. Don't make idle threats about what you'll do if someone's performance doesn't improve. If you escalate a situation, be prepared to do what you say.

HOW DO WE BUILD COURAGE?

How do you build courage if you've lived your life avoiding conflict and playing the peacemaker, or flying off the handle when your emotions overwhelm you? Courage develops with practice and persistence. Courage, like confidence, is a muscle: the more you use it, the stronger it gets and the easier it will be.

Here are a few strategies to help:

USE BODY LANGUAGE TO YOUR ADVANTAGE

Body language and the impact it has on your communication is a huge topic and one that could be the focus of an entire book itself (and, in fact, it is).

Studies show that in face-to-face communication, people read your body language before your words. That doesn't mean your words aren't important – they absolutely are – but it also means you need to focus on ensuring your body language matches the message you're trying to convey.

If you stand confidently in a 'high-power' pose, research says people will perceive you as more confident and competent, even if you're not. But it's not just other people's perceptions that your body language impacts. It's also your own.

Harvard University lecturer and social psychologist Amy Cuddy has studied the impacts of high- and low-power poses over many years. High-power posing involves body language such as standing tall with your feet shoulder width apart, shoulders back, without crossing your arms. Cuddy's research found that, by adopting these expansive postures or 'power poses', people feel more powerful. In short, our body language governs how we think and feel about ourselves.

What does that have to do with courage? Cuddy found that how we hold our bodies can have an impact on our minds. So, if you want to make yourself feel more courageous before a difficult conversation, try adopting a high-power pose for a couple of minutes. I'm not suggesting you walk with hands on hips into your next meeting but I am suggesting you lock yourself in your office, a bathroom cubicle, or get in front of a mirror that morning, stand tall and expansive and tell yourself, 'I've got this'.

If you're interested in learning more on the topic, I recommend watching Amy Cuddy's famous 20-minute TED talk on YouTube, *Your body may shape who you are*, or reading her 2015 book *Presence: Bringing your boldest self to your biggest challenges*.

DRESS FOR THE OCCASION

What you wear will influence how you feel. Choose clothes you feel powerful and comfortable in, provided they are still appropriate for the situation, and you'll feel courageous. Whatever it is for you – a favourite suit or briefcase, a freshly ironed high-vis uniform, an exquisite watch – dress to build your confidence in yourself. This will flow on to your communication.

FAKE IT 'TIL YOU MAKE IT

For many years I trained netball umpires. I was an umpire myself and worked with many new umpires as they learnt how to officiate for the first time. The key piece of advice I gave beginner netball umpires had nothing to do with the rules of netball and everything to do with being confident and courageous. Quite simply, I always told them to fake it 'til they make it.

This advice doesn't only apply on the netball court – it's applicable in your career, business and personal life. Let me be clear: the expression 'fake it 'til you make it' is not about lying or being dishonest. It's not about being inauthentic or exaggerating your skills and abilities. Rather, it's about an attitude. It's about having the courage to act confidently even when you don't feel it and believing in yourself rather than giving into that niggly voice of self-doubt.

Confidence has a significant impact on performance. Look at the world's best athletes. Whether it's tennis stars in a grand slam final, swimmers at the Olympic Games, or soccer players holding their nerve in a penalty shootout, mental preparation and training is as important as physical training. To win, they must believe they can. The same goes for you and your communication. You have to believe you can do the job well.

For a beginner umpire, knowing the rules of netball is important but the courage to be confident is vital. The umpire may feel nervous and unsure of their calls, but they can't let the players see that. If they do – if they blow their whistle softly and make weak, uncertain calls in a soft apologetic voice – the game will get out of hand, fast! If players believe they can intimidate an umpire and potentially impact the calls made, they will. I've seen it happen many times.

However, if an umpire acts confidently, regardless of how nervous and unsure they feel, they command the respect of the players. It doesn't matter if the umpire internally questions every decision they make, as long as they blow their whistle loud and sharp, speak in a strong voice, and make their calls decisively. If the players believe the umpire is confident, they will believe she is competent, even if they don't agree with all of the decisions made.

COURAGE IS THE BY-PRODUCT OF A GOOD PLAN

A plan gives you courage and confidence. This applies to any action you take in life, including both verbal and written communication. When you do the thinking first and consider how to best structure your message, you will gain the courage to deliver it.

As the popular business adage goes, 'failing to plan is planning to fail'. The reason courage is the fourth step in the Five C model is because the preceding Cs – choice, control and consideration – all build on each other to give you the courage to act.

Relying on courage under pressure, without putting those other steps in place first, is like building a house with no foundations and expecting it to withstand a storm. It doesn't make sense.

Behaving confidently, speaking up when you're nervous or afraid, and having a direct conversation when it's not your natural communication style all require courage. But being courageous becomes easier if those founding steps are in place. And once you have built that courage, you're ready – finally – to communicate.

Chapter 9

COMMUNICATION

If this was a standard communication book, this chapter would be at the start. In fact, when you first picked up this book and looked at the contents pages, you might have wondered why the communication chapter was the last in the book! If you've been cheeky and flicked straight here looking for quick tips and strategies before reading the rest of the book, stop right now. Start from the beginning because this chapter will have little impact until you read the rest.

The reason so many people fail at communication is because they jump straight to the communicating without doing the thinking first. They try to build the house without first laying those crucial foundations. They react emotionally and/or automatically without first managing themselves or considering their approach, and then wonder why it doesn't work out. They wonder why their message didn't hit the mark, why no-one listened, why they didn't say what they wanted to say, why they lost their cool and yelled, why they stayed silent and said nothing at all, or why the whole conversation was a train wreck they wished they could take back.

We are all on the lookout for a quick fix – communication hacks that solve our problems and give us skills, tips and tricks to help us improve today, right now. However, when we find these skills are ineffective or short-lived, we are left frustrated, wondering why we can't put them into practice consistently. Instead, we fall back to doing what we've always done.

But that's not you anymore. Having followed the first four Cs outlined in this book, you're now ready to communicate effectively. You've done the prep work. You've made a choice about who you want to be. You're in control of yourself and understand what you can and can't control with others. You've considered the other person and how to shape your communication to give you the best chance of getting the outcome you want. And you've taken a dose of courage and are prepared to have a difficult conversation.

Now it's time to pull it all together. It's time to implement what you've learnt. For many of you, once you've been through the first four steps, your communication will take care of itself. That's the point of this process. If you've built on one step after the other, you're now ready to communicate, even if under immense pressure.

For others, this last step might be a challenge. That's okay. Yes, the foundations are critical, but they won't help until you take the last step and apply them to actual communication. You need to practice. No one else can do it for you. Preparation is important but it's not the same as doing. Thinking is not doing. Knowing is not doing. Only doing is doing.

It's time to take action.

BUILD TRUST WITH WARMTH

We all know the importance of trust in relationships, but how do we build it through our communications?

According to Amy Cuddy, who I mentioned in the previous chapter, the critical factors in communicating effectively to build trust are warmth and kindness. In other words, *how* you communicate is just as important as *what* you communicate.

In the article 'Connect, Then Lead', published by Amy Cuddy, Matthew Kohut and John Neffinger in the July-August 2013 issue of *Harvard Business Review*, beginning with warmth is the way to increase influence. They found that warmth contributes more significantly to others' evaluation of us than competence and strength. Why? Because warmth conveys our underlying intention. It shows the person receiving our communication that we care about them and have their interests at heart – even if the message we're delivering is difficult to hear. Warmth builds respect and if someone respects us, they are more likely to cooperate and align themselves with us.

Unfortunately, warmth tends to get forgotten in times of pressure, such as when we're delivering negative feedback, communicating news of significant change – like a restructure – or in the midst of a crisis. The focus instead is often on projecting strength. In fact, leaders worry that kindness and concern will be seen as weak and soft. The logic seems to be, "Just tell them the facts and keep it cold, direct and specific. That way, they know we're serious and this is the way it's going to be."

I have seen this end very badly, with companies and individual managers accused of being heartless and uncaring. According to Cuddy, Kohut and Neffinger, when strength and competence come before, or without, warmth in your communication, trust is undermined. While people may comply with your instructions publicly, privately they are more likely to disengage, feel resentful and lack respect for you.

That said, strength and competence are still crucial for success. Warmth without these traits can see a person judged as weak, incompetent, and someone to be pitied. You don't want that either. But while strength and competence are important, Cudddy, Kohut and Neffinger argue you should always lead with warmth first.

So, how do you incorporate warmth into your communication?

Some suggestions include:

▸ Showing enthusiasm and genuine interest in the other person.

▸ Using a calm tone and a lower pitch – the sort of style you would use if comforting or confiding in a friend.

▸ Sharing something personal and showing vulnerability to demonstrate your own humanity. This may include admitting a new system has been difficult for you to get your head around too, or acknowledging your own feelings of frustration at delays on a project. Vulnerability fosters trust and respect.

▸ Demonstrating empathy and compassion. Acknowledging people's feelings and concerns.

▸ Addressing the elephant in the room. Showing people you're willing to tackle the heavy and emotional stuff and not just push it aside.

▸ Smiling (and meaning it). A simple smile generates immediate warmth and is not something you can fake successfully. People can tell if you're insincere.

Keep this in mind as you communicate. Are you demonstrating warmth, even when you're frustrated and angry? Do you show that you care and are interested? If you don't seem interested in the person you're communicating with, why should they be interested in what you have to say?

USE 'I' STATEMENTS

Of the many communication strategies that I teach, one of the most powerful is the use of 'I'.

'I' statements allow you to have difficult conversations without sounding aggressive or confrontational. They help you deal with conflict and 'fight fair' by acknowledging what you're saying is your perception/interpretation, rather than an overarching truth.

For example, rather than say "you're wrong", which immediately escalates a situation and often prompts an argument where the other person responds with either, "No I'm not, YOU'RE wrong" or "I'm right", you might instead say, "I disagree". Can you see how that immediately changes the tone? When you lead with an 'I' statement, you're more likely to prompt a conversation where the other person responds with a question, such as, "Why is that?"

Instead of saying "You never listen to me" (perception presented as truth), try, "I feel like my opinion isn't being heard" (perception presented as perception).

'I' statements are also a way of injecting empathy into your communication. Examples include: 'I feel', 'I understand', 'I can tell you're frustrated', 'I can see you're upset'. In addition, they allow you to focus on facts and behaviour rather than making your communication sound like a personal attack, as demonstrated in this basic model for delivering assertive feedback below:

- When you _____ (focus only on the facts or behaviour)
- I feel _____ (this is your perception, interpretation of events, or emotional response)
- Because _____ (you may add some further context here if relevant).
- What I need from you is _____ (ask for what you want or need and then let go of the result).

Reframing 'you' statements into 'I' statements is something you can do quite simply with practice. Once you get used to it, it's something you can do in your head within seconds during a conversation.

Why not put your skills to the test and have a go at reframing the 'you' statements on the following page? Remember, either lead with an 'I' statement or use facts and examples to make your initial point, then add the 'I' statement to highlight your perception.

- You're too aggressive.
- Your work isn't up to scratch.
- You're being unreasonable.
- You never consider my suggestions.
- You should know what I want.
- You need to calm down.

CREATE A SENSE OF UNITY AND SHARED PURPOSE WITH 'WE'.

While 'I' statements are one of the most important tools in your communication toolbox, the use of 'we' also serves an important purpose – particularly for leaders trying to unify, engage and empower a team or workforce.

'We' statements can reduce the feeling of 'us and them' between leaders and staff that can be generated by 'you' statements. They help create shared responsibility, show that you consider yourself part of the team, and convey that you're willing to do yourself what you're asking of others (although it's crucial that your behaviour then backs this up).

For example, you may say: "We are going through a time of disruptive change in our industry and it's a difficult time for all of us," or, "We all need to work extra hard to meet the deadline – me included."

The use of 'we' and 'our' when talking about your company or organisation is also a way of personalising your communications and creating a sense of connection. Rather than saying, "Methmac Communications is committed to helping its clients", go with "We are committed to helping our clients" instead.

A word of warning though: Do not use 'we' as a way of avoiding direct or difficult conversations. Don't use it to diminish your own responsibility (by avoiding 'I') or to avoid addressing a personal concern with an individual. Only use the collective pronoun when you intend to include a group of people – and be sure you really are speaking for a group, rather than yourself. Don't say 'we all think the work Christmas party should be held on a weekend this year', if you're only speaking for yourself and one other colleague amongst a team of 20! This sort of overstatement almost always backfires and demonstrates a lack of courage. It shows you're not prepared to own your opinion or message.

STAY HARD ON THE ISSUE, SOFT ON THE PERSON

Throughout this book, I have spoken about the importance of clear, concise and direct communication that is also empathetic and warm.

This is particularly important when delivering difficult or negative feedback. To have these tough conversations effectively, the key is to stay hard on the issue, soft on the person. If you go soft on the issue, people won't take your feedback seriously. If you go hard on the person, they'll shut down and disengage, or run straight to HR with claims of bullying.

So how do you deliver difficult feedback or a tough message? Well, let me start by telling you what not to do.

One of the most popular approaches for delivering difficult feedback over the last 30 years, taught in many management and communication courses, has been the 'shit sandwich' approach. But in my opinion, in many cases the sandwich approach is just that – shit.

What is the sandwich approach? It's sandwiching negative feedback between two positive points. A slice of praise, the real feedback acting as the meat in the middle, and then another slice of positivity to round it out. Criticism squeezed between compliments. Positive, negative, positive.

The idea behind the sandwich approach is that it softens the blow and protects people's feelings, it encourages and highlights someone's strengths while also suggesting room for improvement. And look, if that's what you're genuinely trying to do, then the sandwich method is appropriate. It's not always shit.

But if the intention of your feedback is to address a serious concern, poor behaviour or a negative performance issue, couching your feedback in praise is not your best bet.

Here are two reasons why:

It's not authentic and feels fake.

The recipient will often see the praise as disingenuous. They know (or think they know) the praise is only there to soften the blow and they resent it. They focus on the negative feedback and discard the positive. They become frustrated and angry you couldn't just tell them what was on your mind and in future they don't believe the compliments you give, feeling that it's a lie. Rather than making the feedback more palatable, your sandwich approach damages your relationship and their trust in you is undermined.

It waters down feedback and detracts from your message.

The opposite can be even more problematic. Rather than discarding the positives that form either end of your sandwich, some people will hold onto them firmly and ignore the 'shit' in the middle – the real feedback you wanted to convey. They gloss over the problem and figure it's not that serious given that you had so many nice things to say as well.

This can lead to the recipient remaining oblivious to the problem or believing it's simply a minor issue and not something that needs immediate attention.

The alternative...

So, if the sandwich approach is on the nose, what is the best way to give feedback?

Well, the first thing to understand is there's not a one-size-fits-all approach. Different people have different personalities, preferences and communication styles, and this will affect the way they like to receive feedback. Some people like their feedback direct, others do like a softer approach.

But either way, when it comes to delivering negative or difficult feedback, the key is to stay hard on the issue and soft on the person. It's about delivering your message in a clear, specific and concise way, while also using tact.

Here are 10 pointers to help you do it well. Some have been covered in previous chapters, but I think it's important to provide you with a practical step-by-step feedback framework for success.

How to give difficult feedback:

1. Inoculate first. Tell the person it's going to be a tough conversation. You might say, "This is going to be a difficult conversation and you may not like what you hear."

2. Set the ground rules for how the conversation will take place: "I know you'll probably have questions, but it's important that you listen to what I have to say first and then you'll have an opportunity to explain things from your point of view."

3. Tell them why you're having the conversation (make it genuine, don't fake it). "The reason we're having this conversation is because you're a valued member of this team and I want you to be successful, which is why I

need to speak with you about the way you communicate with some of your colleagues, because at the moment it's having a negative impact on your relationships."

4. Tell them what it's really about and be specific. Make it about the behaviour, not the person: "I have had a number of people speak with me recently about your communication style being abrupt and aggressive. This has included others within the team and also managers who have been in meetings with you."

5. Provide examples to demonstrate your point. "I have witnessed it myself too. For example, this morning when Katie asked you whether you'd finished the report yet, you snapped back, 'No. You'll get it when it's done,' without even looking up from your computer. It might not have been your intention, but it was perceived by me and others as aggressive."

6. Be empathetic, but firm. "I know you've been under a lot of pressure lately and it's a stressful time of year, but we are a small team and it's important we are able to work together in a respectful way. It's also important that people feel they can communicate openly with you, because otherwise it's going to be difficult for you and them to do your jobs properly."

7. Own your part and take responsibility for your actions. If you should have raised this issue with them weeks ago, tell them that and apologise.

8. Ask for their feedback and thoughts. Although it doesn't excuse poor behaviour, giving the recipient the opportunity to explain any reasons why it occurred is important for gaining a full picture of the situation. It's also important they feel heard.

9. Tell them what change needs to happen and be clear of the consequences. "What I need is for you to be more mindful about your tone and the way you communicate with others. Take the time to explain your reasons if you haven't completed a report and if you do snap, own it and apologise. If you are on a deadline and can't talk, let them know that."

10. Get their commitment and finish with a clear course of action and shared understanding of the conversation. Make sure you're both on the same page and there is no ambiguity. If appropriate, schedule a follow up conversation to track progress in a few weeks' time.

Next time you deliver difficult feedback, throw the sandwich in the bin and try this instead.

FACTS TELL, STORIES SELL

There's an old sales adage I use when teaching people how to better connect with their audience: facts tell, stories sell. This doesn't just apply to sales, it's relevant to any communication. Stories create a human and emotional connection, and it's these connections that drive our decisions. Stories humanise you, which further develops trust and respect. They also bring what you're saying to life and make your message relevant and memorable.

As storytelling expert Gabrielle Dolan says in her 2017 book, *Stories for Work: The Essential Guide to Business Storytelling*, "It's emotion, not logical information that helps us to remember messages."

I have shared stories all the way through this book to help demonstrate the strategies I'm talking about and illustrate what I'm saying in a practical way. These stories allow you to see the skills I'm teaching in action and help you connect with my messages more strongly. It would have been a dry and boring book without them.

I also share personal stories in all my workshops. I speak openly about the challenges of my husband's depression and share insights into my own weaknesses and failures. I don't do this because my stories are remarkable – I share them to connect with my audience and remind them that I'm human too.

It shows that my content is authentic and real. Sharing my stories tells people why they should listen to me and why what I teach has credibility – because I apply these skills to my own life and highlight this through examples. I notice people pay more attention when I share my stories. People lean forward in their chairs. Heads nod. Everyone listens intently to hear what I say next. By doing this, I make my content relevant to others. By showing them how I apply the skills in my own life, they can see how they can apply them in theirs too.

You don't need to tell long stories. In fact, it's better if they're not. The last thing you want to do is ramble. Keep your stories short, sharp, real, relevant and relatable. And most important of all – make sure they serve a purpose. Don't simply tell stories for stories' sake, at least, not in the workplace.

Stories can be added to any communication. Even a dry monthly financial report can be made more engaging with stories. You saved $10,000 last month – great! Bring it to life by telling your audience what that equates to. What could you buy with that money? What does it mean for your business?

IF IN DOUBT, ASK

Sometimes, even after implementing the first four Cs, you'll still feel nervous about using them when you communicate. This is particularly so if you're about to disagree with someone who is in a position of power over you.

Perhaps your boss has introduced a new way of doing a task. You've tried it their way, but it didn't work. Now you have to tell them. Although you have already considered the risk of speaking up and decided the risk of staying silent is greater, you're still worried about the impact your words will have on your career or future relationship with that person.

In this case, a good tactic is to start the conversation by asking the person if they're happy for you to provide feedback or a different opinion. Yes, it's deferential but often this simple one- or two-liner to preface your question or opinion can make the difference between your boss receiving your message well and considering it rude insubordination.

You might say: "Amy, I'm wondering if I could give you some feedback about the new registration process. I've tried the new system a few times now and I wanted to talk through my experience with you. Are you happy for me to do that?" Like the inoculate-first concept that I introduced in Chapter 7, this kind of introduction can be a game changer.

FOLLOW UP

Once you've had a difficult conversation, it's tempting to think your job is done, but the best communicators know the high-pressure conversation is not the end of the story. If you want to maintain your relationship with a person, it's important that you continue to communicate with them regularly and follow up after a difficult conversation has been had.

Make an effort to check in with them in the days and weeks afterwards, when the pressure drops off. If your conversation was about something like a restructure or redundancy, check to see how they're travelling and whether there's anything you can do to help. If the conversation was about poor performance or an expected change in behaviour, see how they're going at putting the changes in place.

It's also important to seek out conversations with the person that aren't fraught – ask them about their family, talk footy, or anything else that shows you care about them as a person. This effort to maintain communication will allow you both to move on or ask further questions; demonstrates your warmth, maturity and strength as a leader; and will make the next difficult conversation that much easier, because you will have proven you can communicate effectively under pressure without falling into deny, blame, justify and defend.

THE FIVE CS IN ACTION

Now you've learnt about The Five Cs of Effective Communication – choice, control, consideration, courage and communication - let's take a look at how they can all come together.

Belinda knew she had to have a difficult conversation with Tim. She'd avoided it for as long as she could. Tim was a friend, but he was also an employee in her wellness business, and he wasn't performing. He was often late for appointments with his massage clients, talked excessively about his personal life during treatments, and lacked enthusiasm.

A number of clients spoke to Belinda about his behaviour but when bookings started dropping off, Belinda knew she had to act. She had tried to address Tim's performance in a roundabout way, talking to him about the experience they collectively provided through the business and the level of service their clients expected. The problem was, while Tim agreed enthusiastically with Belinda during these conversations, his behaviour didn't reflect what he said. He seemed to lack self-awareness about his actions and the impact they were having on the business.

Belinda came to me for a one-on-one coaching session, upset but determined to work out how to address the issue directly with Tim. We went through the Five Cs and by the end of our session, Belinda had made a conscious choice to take personal responsibility for the conversation and the way she wanted to handle it. She knew staying in control would be difficult because of their friendship and came to terms with the fact she would have no control over Tim's reaction to her feedback, she could only control herself. Next, we moved onto consideration. How would Belinda frame the conversation? What was it actually about? And when would be the best time and place to deliver it? To help give her the courage to have the conversation, Belinda and I worked through the three questions – what's the worst that could happen, what would be the reality if it did happen, and how could she mitigate the worst-case scenario from eventuating? All that was left was for Belinda to have the conversation.

Belinda chose the end of a business day to speak with Tim because if afforded them privacy and she started the conversation by acknowledging the complexity of their relationship.

"I need to have a conversation with you about your performance that's going to be awkward for both of us because we're friends as well as colleagues," Belinda began. "But because we are friends and I respect you personally and professionally, it's even more important that I address these issues with you because I want us to continue working together for many years to come."

After giving Tim the why of the conversation, Belinda outlined her expectations for how the discussion would go. "I'm sure you'll want to have your say on this, but I ask that you please listen to my points first and then you'll have the opportunity to respond..." This was important as their friendship could have otherwise blurred the lines of employer/employee and led to Tim interrupting.

Belinda outlined the specific concerns she had about Tim's performance. She kept it factual and gave clear examples but delivered the information with warmth, finishing with a question to show she cared.

"I know you pride yourself on your professionalism and this behaviour is really not like you, so the first thing I want to ask is – is everything okay?"

Although Tim was upset and defensive, he confessed to being stressed about the upcoming birth of his first child and how he would provide for his family once his partner stopped work. Belinda empathised with him about his concerns but stayed firmly focused on the issue.

She clearly articulated her expectations about Tim's performance: he must be on time for all appointments, keep personal conversations on client arrival friendly but minimal, and refrain from conversation during massage sessions. She ended the conversation by outlining future steps. She told Tim they would meet again in two weeks for a follow-up discussion to see how things were progressing and encouraged him to speak with someone outside of work about his fears of becoming a father.

When I checked in with Belinda a few weeks later, she told me Tim had decided to change careers and accepted a higher-paying job that would better support his expanding family. While she was disappointed to lose a staff member, Belinda said the conversation about his performance was the catalyst for Tim to analyse his life and the direction he was headed, which had resulted in a win for both of them.

"If I hadn't had that conversation, his performance would probably have kept declining, I would have lost more clients, it would have affected our friendship, and my business would have suffered too," Belinda said. "Instead, I've saved our friendship and my business. Some of the clients that had left have come back and made new bookings. I've had some great applications for a new masseuse and I now feel like I'm more in control of where my business is going and how I want it to run. Tim thanked me for being such an understanding boss and friend, and we're catching up for dinner this weekend."

Communication – the final piece in the Five C puzzle – meant Belinda was able to have a very difficult conversation under high pressure, with the best outcome possible. And it can do the same for you too.

COMMUNICATION IS A PROCESS, NOT AN END GAME

Communication isn't something you do once and then it's over. It's not something you save for difficult conversations when you're forced to take action because the pressure has built up. It's a daily action – essential if you want to maintain and improve your personal and professional relationships. Communication should be something you do regularly, openly, authentically and warmly; something you include as part of your everyday routine, much like brushing your teeth.

Done well, communication will stave off conflict and the need for many high-pressure conversations. People will know where you stand and, as a result, where they stand. You remove assumptions and mitigate uncertainty when you communicate clearly, which then allows for increased productivity and efficiency. If everyone knows where they're going and what page they're starting from, they can get on with their job and get there quicker.

Remember, communication is much more than speaking. Body language and listening are just as important. It's a mistake to focus on having a difficult conversation and nothing else. Make listening – really listening – part of your everyday communication practice. Breathe deeply, quieten your internal chatter and listen to what is – and isn't – being said around you. Not only will you learn more about how people feel and what's going on, but you'll also be better placed to have a considered, controlled and courageous conversation because you have all the information in front of you.

CONCLUSION

No one gets it right all the time. Communication is not something you'll ever perfect. But before you throw this book in the air shouting, "Then what's the bloody point?!", let me reiterate what I said at the start – no one is a perfect communicator; everyone can improve. It doesn't matter whether you're the CEO or a new starter, you can always do better. Be humble enough to recognise this, self-aware enough to know the areas you need to work on, and persistent enough to strive for continual improvement.

I'm a communications specialist and I get it wrong all the time. But I'm always trying to improve. One of the reasons I love teaching the steps, strategies and techniques outlined in this book is because every time I do – whether it's through writing this book, delivering a workshop, or coaching a client – it gives me a kick in the butt to lift my own game. We can always do better; every single one of us.

So where should you start? How do you work to improve your communication without being overwhelmed by the complexity and magnitude of it all? How do you stop it from feeling like too much hard work and that perhaps soft skills are just *too* hard after all?

Start by taking a deep breath. It's okay. You're not going to try to do everything at once. Remember that neuroplasticity stuff in Chapter 3? You can do this. You can rewire your brain. Yes, improving your communication skills on a consistent basis *will* be hard work initially and it will take time. You're not going to undo 20, 30, or 40-plus years of natural tendencies and bad habits in one day, one month, or even one year. It's not going to magically happen for you the minute you get to the end of this book. So how do you get to where you want to be?

Commit to making a change

Commit to following the Five Cs in order – choice, control, consideration, courage, communication - with each progressive step building on the one before it. As you start to master one, you'll naturally flow onto the next and each step will gradually become easier. Make a choice about who you are and who you want to be, and get conscious of whether you're operating from a fixed or growth mindset. Try to stay above the line and in The Empowerment Dynamic (explained in Chapter 5) as much as possible.

Work on your emotional intelligence. Increase your self-awareness and work on regulating your emotions so you are more in control of your communications. Once you have greater control, you'll be able to put more consideration into your approach.

Consider the outcome you want and the best way to get it after thinking about your audience, context, situation and circumstance. This will give you the courage and bravery to finally communicate. And then do it. Have a conversation.

Get conscious

Before you even try to change the way you communicate, take notice of how you communicate now. Get into the habit of reflecting on your interactions with people. Be honest with yourself. Consider what you do and don't say, and how well you listen.

Ask yourself if what you did was the best way of handling it. Could you have done better? If so, how?

A great way to improve your consciousness is to start a communication journal. It need not be arduous – just a few lines each evening about your day's communications and how you think they went. The key is getting yourself into the habit of regular reflection.

Start small

Improving your communication is a big project. You will make mistakes and feel uncomfortable. If you have blamed other people for making you communicate aggressively all your life, you won't suddenly stop. If you try to implement everything at once, you may become despondent and feel overwhelmed.

As you would with any big project, break it down into manageable chunks, and then break them down further into tangible actions. Start small because developing a new skill takes time. Pick one or two things to focus on before moving onto the next. Perhaps it'll be reducing your use of the word 'just' as an apology word, or putting a pause between your reaction and response. Whatever it is, work on improving it before moving onto the next.

Be accountable

I know this is scary, but if you're genuinely committed to improving your communication, I encourage you to tell someone. Being accountable to yourself is important but being accountable to someone else takes it to another level. It makes everything more real.

Accountability to yourself is great when things are going well but when it all gets a bit too hard, it's too easy to pretend like you never made a commitment in the first place. 'Let me just quietly pretend like I never read that silly communications book,' your ego whispers. 'No one will ever know.'

So, tell someone. Tell them you're working to improve your communication skills and ask them to check in on how you're going. Ask them for feedback to see if they notice any improvement.

Be selective in who you ask, though. Choosing an accountability buddy is something to consider carefully. You want someone who is going to be honest with you, who's going to support and champion you. But you also want someone who's going to challenge you to persevere through the difficult times and won't let you quit if it all gets too hard.

You're looking for someone who operates from The Empowerment Dynamic themselves. Someone who is a challenger, coach and creator all rolled into one. It might be a friend or family member. It might be a mentor or colleague. It might not be someone in your inner circle at all.

Some of the best accountability buddies are those who are not part of your everyday life, and not too worried about hurting your feelings. If you know someone else who has read this book, why not make them your accountability buddy? Or, if you ask someone else, send them a copy of the book so they understand what you're trying to achieve. Check in with them regularly – make it a weekly appointment – and note how you're both tracking.

Persistence and practice pay

Motivation is fleeting – it gets you started but wanes and eventually dissipates. Habit will keep you going. To make real and lasting change you have to be ferociously persistent. You have to persevere, even when it feels too hard. The best way to improve your communication is to practice. While doing the thinking first is crucial, it's not putting your newly learnt skills and strategies into action. The more you practice the steps in this book, the easier they'll become. Like any skill, you get better at it the more you do it.

Start by practicing in low-threat, low-stakes environments, like giving timely, direct and honest feedback next time a staff member submits a report, and then move up and test your skills in more pressurised situations. Eventually, if you don't give up, these steps will become second nature and you'll do them without even thinking. The Five Cs will underpin every interaction and conversation you have, and you'll move through them within seconds in your head. You won't always achieve the outcome you want but you will have the best chance of achieving success. What is success? In my experience, it means knowing you did everything you could to communicate in the best way possible and letting the chips fall where they may.

SOFT IS THE NEW HARD

Soft is the new hard. It's as simple as that. The people bit is the hardest part of our professional and personal lives, and it's only heightened when there's pressure involved.

Before you go, I want to give you some parting words of advice to help you on your way, because finishing this book is just the beginning – now it's time to get to work.

Not only will following the steps outlined in this book improve your communication and interpersonal relationships, it will also improve you and your life. When you learn to manage yourself under pressure, you'll be less stressed, more resilient, more in control, and a hell of a lot more powerful. You'll be highly respected and trusted. You'll be seen as a leader and be more likely to receive promotional opportunities. You'll achieve better outcomes in every area of your life, both personal and professional. But only if you do the work.

Some people will resist your attempts to change, particularly if the strategies you put in place are new behaviours for you. Those people who have pushed you around in the past will not like you standing up for yourself. Those people who are used to you responding aggressively might be confused by or suspicious of your newfound calmness. Don't worry. They'll get used to it. You may even decide to be honest and tell them about your effort to communicate better so they understand the change in style.

There will be times when you're tempted to fall back into old habits – you're trying to change the way you've communicated for years. Personal responsibility is hard. It's easier to blame other people. But you are in control of your life and, if the biggest roadblock to your success is you, you also have the ability to get out of your own way. Let that empower, inspire and excite you to take action, because taking action will change everything.

I long for a world in which people take control of the way they communicate and, as a result, the success in their lives. I hope that with what you've learnt in these pages you're now ready to be part of the growing community of people who are doing that.

Life's not a practice run. This is it. Get out of your own way and step up for success.

BE PART OF A COMMUNITY
OF GREAT COMMUNICATORS

As I've mentioned throughout this book, I welcome feedback, so I invite you to get in touch with me to share your thoughts and questions, plus your success after implementing the Five Cs in your life.

You can reach me through my website at leahmether.com.au or connect with me on social media.

I also offer organisational training, one-on-one and team coaching, facilitation and keynote presentations. Visit my website to find out more.

I hope to meet you in person soon.

Leah.

THE FIVE Cs OF EFFECTIVE COMMUNICATION

CHOICE > CONTROL > CONSIDERATION > COURAGE > COMMUNICATION

ACKNOWLEDGEMENTS

This book is one of my proudest achievements. It was written in the cracks, around a thriving business and three energetic little boys, during one of the most challenging periods of my life.

Seeing my hard work, persistence, determination, late nights and early mornings reflected in these pages gives me an overwhelming sense of joy and satisfaction. It proves that with a strong goal, detailed plan, discipline and personal drive, almost anything is possible.

But I didn't get this book to where it is on my own.

First, I'd like to thank my friend Maree McPherson for referring me to Kath Walters, the editor and book coach extraordinaire who helped guide me through the book planning, writing and publishing process.

Knowing I needed to make best use of my limited time, I approached Kath for support and advice before I wrote a word. With Kath's guidance, probing questions, and honest feedback, I knew exactly what I had to do and not a second was wasted during the writing process. Kath's editing prowess also helped shape my manuscript into the finished product you have today.

This book contains references to the works of many great thought leaders. In particular I'd like to acknowledge the models and concepts of the Global Leadership Foundation, Stephen Karpman, David Emerald, Rachael Robertson, Oscar Trimboli, Daniel Goleman, Viktor Frankl and Stephen Covey.

These pages also include many stories and anecdotes from a wide range of clients; leaders who have shared their fears, failures and insecurities with me over many years. Although I have changed their names and identifying details, their stories are real. Thank you all for your questions, vulnerability and desire to improve your communication. It was you who inspired the Five C model and the content of this book.

To my team – Kate and Efriel – thank you for helping me create space in my business to write.

To my first readers, Ami Summers, Amy Dynes, Kate Blain, Kate Mether, Katie Grima, Rachael Law, Kelly Mether, Maree McPherson, Marg Mether, Ron Mether, Sally Neenan and Robyn Wildblood – thank you for generously giving me your time and valuable feedback during your summer holidays. It was so hugely appreciated.

Late in my writing process, I had the sudden realisation that I needed to rebrand my company before the book was released. To this end I'd like to thank the talented Zach Jacobs from Imprint Marketing + Design for his great work to create a new look and feel for brand Leah Mether.

Zach's branding informed the work of my incredible book designer, Liz Seymour from Seymour Designs, who nailed the cover design on the first go. Thanks Liz. Although it's not the '17 Storey Treehouse' style cover my son hoped for, it's exactly what I was after.

In addition to being available in hard copy and e-book, Soft is the New Hard is also available as an audiobook, thanks to the help of Dave Stokes from Author2Audio. Shoutout to Build Live Give founder Paul Higgins for his Corporate Escapees podcast on which I first heard Dave speak.

And last but not least, to my family and friends. How lucky am I to have such an incredible tribe in my corner cheering me on?

To my parents, Ron and Marg, words are inadequate to express how grateful I am for the foundations you laid for me and the support and guidance you continue to give me today. This book contains many of the lessons you taught me growing up. When I write about leading by example, that's exactly what you both did. Thank you.

To my brilliant sisters, Kelly, Rachael and Jessica. Thank you for always being there. I can always count on you to have my back and give it to me straight.

To Mia. Thanks for being awesome. You're my rock and a wonderful friend.

To my husband Tim. We've been through a lot. Thank you for understanding my late nights and early mornings in front of the computer when I should have been in bed and sorry for all the times I woke you up. I love you.

Finally, to my sons – Sam, Callum and Lucas. I hope I'm giving you the foundations to be happy and successful in life and that one day you read this book and it helps guide you through. I love you to bits.

www.ingramcontent.com/pod-product-compliance
Lightning Source LLC
Chambersburg PA
CBHW061020220326
41597CB00016BB/1751